Act Justly,
Love Mercifully,
and Walk Humbly
with Your God

Act Justly, Love Mercifully, and Walk Humbly with Your God

Father Don McNeill, C.S.C., and Margaret Pfeil

Andrews McMeel
Publishing®

a division of Andrews McMeel Universal

We dedicate this book to all who have been formed and shaped through the Community for the International Lay Apostolate (CILA), the programs of the Center for Social Concerns (CSC), the Holy Cross Associates (HCA), and the Holy Cross Mission Center.

Contents

Introduction

Fr. Don McNeill, C.S.C., and Margaret Pfeil

This priceless treasure we hold, so to speak, in a common earthenware jar—to show that the splendid power of it belongs to God and not to us. We are handicapped on all sides, but we are never frustrated; we are puzzled, but never in despair. We are persecuted, but we never have to stand it alone: we may be knocked down but we are never knocked out! Every day we experience something of the death of the Lord Jesus, so that we may also know the power of the life of Jesus in these bodies of ours. (2 Corinthians 4:7–10)[1]

On a beautiful, sunny day in early 1988, we recalled this passage from 2 Corinthians together as we sat on a bench at St. George's, a K–12 school in Santiago, Chile, run by the Congregation of Holy Cross. I (Margie) had just arrived in Chile the previous October to begin two years as a Holy Cross Associate, and the initial landing had been rocky. The last five people "to be disappeared" by the Pinochet regime had been abducted just before our arrival, exacerbating

---

1   I (Don McNeill) prefer this J.B. Phillips version of 2 Cor. 4:7–10 and particularly the phrase "We may be knocked down, but we are never knocked out!"

tensions in the country and heightening the suffocating fear born of fourteen years of dictatorship. On a personal level, when Sylvia Elixavide, Bill Cavanaugh, and I stepped off the plane in Santiago, fresh from language school in Cuernavaca, Mexico, our hearts sank as we quickly realized that we would need at least another two months of immersion in Chilean Spanish before we would be able to communicate beyond a rudimentary level with our neighbors. I was entering a time of spiritual desert.

On the bench that day, Don encouraged me to embrace the fragility and vulnerability of that season of life, an enduring piece of spiritual wisdom that continues to nourish both of us. To this day, nearly every time we meet, we remember that we hold our treasure in clay jars and laugh at the latest reminders of our respective fragility.

In summer 2015, Don called to ask whether I would be willing to work with him on a book. Thus, the present volume began to take shape, with the generous and enthusiastic contributions of many. As has characterized Don's fifty years of priesthood, the book he envisioned could be nurtured only in community. This book springs from the countless personal relationships Don has cultivated as a Holy Cross religious utterly devoted to involving as many people as possible in the work of the Congregation of Holy Cross in service of the church's mission in the world. Don wanted to explore the story of this communal ministerial journey and its fruits.

More than fifty years ago, the Second Vatican Council articulated the significance of the baptismal call to discipleship for all believers, emphasizing active participation of the laity in the life of the church in the world. Responding to that urging, the Congregation of Holy Cross dedicated itself to intentional formation of the laity through academic study of theology and through long-term immersion at its apostolates in the United States, Peru, Chile, and Uganda, among other places. The Center for Social Concerns, founded by Don and a few collaborators at the University of Notre Dame in 1983, deepened these efforts through a combination of pastoral theology, community-based learning, and lay formation for mission.

This volume offers a glimpse of that Vatican II vision seen through the lens of particular narratives. And, for every personal experience recounted here, there are thousands more that remain untold. We lament that we were not able to include them all. We dedicate this book to all who have been formed and shaped through the Community for the International Lay Apostolate (CILA), the programs of the Center for Social Concerns (CSC), the Holy Cross Associates (HCA), and the Holy Cross Mission Center.

"And what does the Lord require of you? To act justly and to love mercy and to walk humbly with your God." (Micah 6:8)[2]

Don has enfleshed this passage from Micah: generations of his students have been formed by bringing these words to life and accepting Don's gentle but persistent invitations to live into them as part of Christian discipleship. This text greeted all who entered the original CSC building, and it is artfully inscribed on a silk scarf in the current CSC coffeehouse, reproduced on the jacket of this book.

Each chapter in some way reflects the spiritual fruit born of trying and often failing to act justly, love mercifully, and walk humbly with God. Bill Cavanaugh recalls a friend wishing him well as he left for Chile, while adding that it would probably be better for him if he failed. Lou Nanni remembers his baptism by fire as a rookie teacher in Santiago. Indeed, a connecting thread running through all these narratives is the tremendously formative experience of reaching the limits of one's capacities and vulnerabilities and finding God there, within oneself and in textured layers of community—the Congregation of Holy Cross, the Associate households, the local

---

2   New International Version.

community of friends and coworkers, and the Body of Christ that is the church, at once scarred and resurrected.

Begin by considering the first two chapters together. The first essay by Andrea Smith Shappell and Felicia Johnson O'Brien offers a fine overview of Don's ministerial life and the ways in which it has yielded so many beautiful fruits, not least in the ongoing work of the CSC. Read in tandem with Maureen O'Brien's piece, it provides the overarching historical context of the book. Maureen carefully articulates the significance of Vatican II for opening up greater possibilities for the sort of lay formation pursued through CILA. It paved the way for Don's efforts to invite students to correlate their immersion experiences with theological reflection, particularly through theology courses using the method of community-based learning.

As Barbara Frey's essay details, Don enthusiastically enlisted many collaborators along the way, including Henri Nouwen, Msgr. Jack Egan, and Peggy Roach, graciously building ties of relationship between students and activists working in inner cities. As those engaged in urban ministry came to campus for conferences and times of respite, Don invited them, along with committed faculty, to share their wisdom with young lay students wrestling with questions of faith, justice, and vocation.

The Urban Plunge and summer immersion placements took shape through these connections, facilitated through the pastoral efforts of Sr. Judith Anne Beattie, C.S.C.; Mary Ann Roemer; Marilyn Bellis; Dee Schlotfeldt; and other colleagues. They began working with Don in the Office of Volunteer Services in 1976, sharing an unobtrusive space in 1.5 LaFortune that only a truly persevering student could manage to find, as Stacy Hennessy attests. By emphasizing the interrelationship of service, justice education, theological reflection, and prayer, they encouraged students to notice the connections between contemplation and action and to discern how God might be drawing them vocationally. Immersion experiences like that of Charlie Kenney in Peru paved the way for the establishment of the HCA program, and Mary Ann walked with students through the application and placement process.

Matt Feeney bears witness to the lasting formative impact of Mary Ann's accompaniment and of his time in HCA. Mary Ellen Konieczny's review of HCA materials through the program's twenty-eight years of existence resonates with Matt's narrative, showing how the HCA pillars of prayer, service, community, and simple living shaped the lives and vocational paths of those involved, not least through the active involvement of members of the Congregation of Holy Cross.

Stacy Hennessy's chapter recounts the path leading to the establishment of the Center for Social Concerns: at Don's invitation, she, along with Mary Meg McCarthy and others, worked to make a case for establishing the CSC in the building being vacated by the WNDU radio station. Backed by a sympathetic and encouraging Fr. Hesburgh, their entreaty to the board of trustees led to the inauguration of the CSC in 1983.

As the HCA program was ending, Paul Mitchell took up an invitation from the Holy Cross Mission Center in 2007 to work with their apostolates in eastern Uganda through the Overseas Lay Missioner Program. Having been shaped significantly by CSC programs and immersion opportunities as an undergraduate, he describes well the disorienting transition into living the lay vocation without the benefit of more structured formation, like that of the novitiate in religious communities. What sort of formation is appropriate and necessary for laypeople entering young adulthood in a fragmented world?

Paul's question lingers and points to the open-endedness of the overarching narrative of this volume. For its part, the CSC has grown from humble roots between floors in LaFortune in an enterprise anchored by four people to spacious new accommodations in Geddes Hall where a staff of more than forty continue to accompany students in linking theory and praxis, faith and justice, contemplation and action. Matt Feeney writes of his "bucket list" desire to re-establish some version of the HCA program, perhaps under the title that Don McNeill suggested, "Companions on Mission."

Fifty years after Vatican II, what might lay collaboration with Holy Cross in service of the church's mission look like? How might the vocational paths of lay and religious contribute to a mutually formative experience of being companions on mission? Come, Holy Spirit!

That these essays surface such questions for discernment is a testament to Don's vision and ministry. He did not want this book to be a Festschrift in his honor, and so the contributors have respected his wish; yet, it is impossible to enter into these narratives without appreciating the profoundly formative influence Don has lovingly exercised in all of our lives. The authors have undertaken this project together as an expression of our deep gratitude for his life and witness among us. He truly has been a companion who invited all of us on mission with him. *¡Gracias, Padre Don!*

CHAPTER 1

Walking Humbly with God: Vatican II after Fifty Years and the Center for Social Concerns after Thirty Years

Andrea Smith Shappell and Felicia Johnson O'Brien

*You have been told, O mortal, what is good, and what the
Lord requires of you: Only to do justice and to love goodness,
and to walk humbly with your God.* (Micah 6:8)

*I*n the Old Testament book of Micah, God chastises the people
of Israel for their corrupt ways and pleads with them to convert.
The Center for Social Concerns (CSC) at the University of Notre
Dame finds its roots in this call to conversion, "to do justice and to
love goodness, and to walk humbly with your God." *Gaudium et Spes*,
a document that emerged from the Second Vatican Council in 1965,
echoes this call to discover God's will on the journey in contemporary
times. Inspired by these mandates, Don McNeill, C.S.C., with Judith
Anne Beattie, C.S.C., and others, founded the Center for Social
Concerns in 1983.

Fifty years after Vatican II, this call continues to inspire the work
of the CSC. Prior to Vatican II, the church utilized a hierarchical
model, one that worked from the top down and rarely employed input
from the laity. In contrast, the documents promulgated in Vatican II

stressed a more symbiotic relationship between the church and the world. It urged more participation from the laity, from all peoples, and from all cultures.[3] The model of community-based learning, which recognizes that all parties benefit from acts of service, also mirrors the shift in thinking that occurred after Vatican II. The notion of inclusivity, of reaching out to all of humankind,[4] further encourages CSC programming to reach an incredibly diverse population in the local, national, and international spheres. By focusing on the church in the world, we as a church, and at the CSC in particular, have an ongoing responsibility to respond to the signs of the times by listening closely to current events, educating ourselves and our students about current social issues, and, finally, advocating on behalf of those who are most affected by injustice in the modern world.

As we reflect upon the roots of the CSC preceding 1983, it is also important to review Don McNeill's formation and the deep influence of Vatican II. As an undergraduate at Notre Dame, Don spent much of his time on the basketball court and in student government activities. After his graduation from Notre Dame in 1958, he and his brother participated in an Institute for European Studies semester in Vienna. While there, Don took a life-changing course with Victor Frankl, discussing ideas that would later become Frankl's book *Man's Search for Meaning*. At the end of the semester, Don went to India, where he was exposed to poverty in a way he had never seen. These two experiences, each confronting suffering, were instrumental in leading him to his vocation as a priest.

Don studied in Rome as a seminarian from 1962 to 1966, coinciding with Vatican II. The church's shift to embrace society more fully made a strong impression on him, particularly the emphasis on addressing the disparity between first-world and third-world countries, integrating local culture in the celebration of liturgy,

---

3 *Gaudium et Spes*, 44.
4 *Gaudium et Spes*, 54–55.

and increasing lay participation in the life of the church. He reflected that the document *Gaudium et Spes* "gave many of us great hope that compassion and justice-related responses to, and with, the suffering of the poor were constitutive components of the Gospel."[5] In other words, the most basic and important work of the church asked that all of its members act with compassion and justice in the world. He carried this vision back to Notre Dame, where he founded the Center for Experiential Learning in 1971.

Don's courses, Theology and Community Service (TCS) and Theology and Social Ministry (TSM), were foundational for hundreds of students from the 1970s to 2002. Don's pastoral theological pedagogy required students to form relationships with the marginalized in the local community and invited students to reflect on their experiences through journal writing. In class, Don facilitated discussion to help students integrate their experiences in the community with their insights from the course readings. Eventually, these types of courses came to be known as service-learning or community-based learning courses that flourish at the Center for Social Concerns to this day.

GETTING TO KNOW FR. DON

ANDREA: As a sophomore at Notre Dame, I enrolled in the course Theology and Community Service on the advice of friends who had taken the course. I was very shy and challenged myself to be in a small group discussion course that included weekly visits to two women in a nursing home. The process of visiting, writing a journal about the visits, responding to theological readings of the course, and discussing the visits and readings with seven peers was life-changing for me.

---

5   Don McNeill's reflection, April 2002.

My faith became alive, and I looked for more opportunities to take courses from Don and to become involved with the student group CILA (see chapter 2 by Maureen O'Brien).

Formed in the integration of faith and action as an undergraduate "groupie" of Don McNeill, I worked in family ministry with Catholic Charities of Gary, Indiana, and then with the social apostolate in New Orleans, Louisiana. I returned to Notre Dame to study for a master's degree in theology and asked Don whether there was a part-time position at the Center for Experiential Learning. Don persuaded me to consider a full-time position that was available, so I decided to take the position coordinating the summer service projects and participating on his teaching teams while pursuing the degree part-time.

I was on the teaching team for Don's experiential learning courses for twenty years. He was a master of inviting four to six people each year to teach with him, allowing much of the classroom time for small group discussions. Don's teaching style offered students a classroom that cultivated the integration of learning from the actions of service with the knowledge from books and lectures. For the following seven years, I worked with students discerning postgraduate service. Now, I direct the Summer Service Learning Program and lead efforts related to theological reflection at the CSC. We still use Don's pastoral theological pedagogy in the Summer Service Learning Program, a three-credit course in theology for approximately two hundred twenty-five students taught by a teaching team of twenty facilitators.

FELICIA: After graduating from Notre Dame in 1995, I helped start a community-based organization and orphanage in Honduras called Farm of the Child. In 1998, at Don's prompting, I took a job working at the admissions office of Notre Dame to focus on recruiting efforts in Latin America. I later pursued my master's in social work at Catholic University in Washington, DC, where I subsequently worked as a social worker with immigrants. Eight years ago, I joined the staff at the Center for Social Concerns as a program director with the Summer Service Learning Program. Personally and professionally, Don continues to accompany me along the different stages of life from college student to professional, wife, and mother.

I didn't really get to know Fr. Don, "Padre," until my senior year at Notre Dame in 1994. My friend Katie Glynn and I were both greatly impacted by our summer service projects and needed a place to process our experiences. Don invited us to meet with him in his dorm room every other week for breakfast. We would stock up with food at the dining hall, bring it to his dorm room, and enjoy coffee and conversation before heading to class. Typically, we shared Mass together around his coffee table along with our photos of friends from the Dominican Republic, Phoenix, and Chile. We honored their lives and struggles and our friendships with them by praying *with* them during the Mass, unified in the Eucharist. How is it that we as twenty-one-year-olds felt like equals with this highly educated priest and executive director of the CSC? How blessed were we to be able to open our hearts to each other in genuine conversation? What a unique experience and gift for me as a young woman to befriend a priest who modeled a life of vulnerability, compassion, and justice and who saw Christ right in front of us, alongside us.

Through our friendship with Don McNeill, Don profoundly influenced our lives and challenged us to be active members and leaders in the church and world. We are deeply grateful to him for the many gifts of his friendship and humbled by the opportunity to write about the ways he has impacted us and so many others through his work at the CSC. Similarly, the Center for Social Concerns played a vital role in our own formations, so much so that we have committed our careers to its ongoing work and growth. Here we would like to explore three themes from Vatican II that stand out in

Don McNeill's teaching and administration and in the overall life of the Center for Social Concerns: embracing the world by listening to and responding to the signs of the times, empowering the laity, and advocating for justice.

RESPONDING TO THE SIGNS OF THE TIMES

As director of the Center for Experiential Learning (1974–1982) and later the Center for Social Concerns (1983–2002), Don invited students and coworkers to read the signs of the times by participating in programs based in the local South Bend community, across the country, and throughout the world. Don's vision was informed by the often-quoted passage from *Gaudium et Spes*, "the Church has always had the duty of scrutinizing the signs of the times and of interpreting them in the light of the Gospel . . . We must therefore recognize and understand the world in which we live, its expectations, its longings, and its often dramatic characteristics."[6] This attempt to "understand the world we live in" is evidenced in the variety of courses taught at the CSC that prioritize immersion, displacement, building relationships with those who are suffering or marginalized, and reflection.

Vatican II began a conversation that invited inquiry and boldness—two qualities that Fr. Don McNeill possessed and passed along to the ethos of the Center for Social Concerns. Vatican II did not address all questions and left certain topics such as family life, marriage, war, and others open to discussion.[7] While these topics were left unresolved, they implicitly began an open conversation about complicated and often contentious issues. The CSC does not shy

---

6   *Gaudium et Spes*, preface, 4.
7   Edna McDonagh, "The Church in the Modern World (*Gaudium et Spes*)," in *Modern Catholicism: Vatican II and After*, ed. Adrian Hastings (Oxford: Oxford University Press, 1991), 97.

away from these issues; seminars,[8] in particular, tackle difficult social concerns that reflect the signs of the times. The center asks students to engage in current issues to discover God's truth revealed here in our midst, the ongoing story of Christ's presence with us. Vatican II "called for an incarnation of Catholic Christianity in the variety of the world's cultures."[9] In response to this incarnation, the CSC seeks to find ways to know and love Christ in the contemporary world.

Don encouraged students and colleagues to respond to the signs of the times, particularly related to poverty, by inviting them to consider opportunities that they might not consider on their own. Stepping out of one's comfort zone and feeling a sense of displacement opened one's eyes and senses to new and difficult realities. Don knew the power of displacement from his own immersion experiences in India and Latin America. Together with Henri Nouwen and Doug Morrison, he wrote the book *Compassion: A Reflection on the Christian Life* as a way to look more deeply at the Christian call to respond with compassion to the social issues of the 1980s. The authors define displacement as a key component of compassion, "going directly to those people and places where suffering is most acute and building a home there."[10] This was the challenge that CSC courses offered to students. As students joined community organizing efforts in Oakland, California, or shared liturgy in a *población* in Chile, the etymology of compassion, the Latin *pati cum*, meaning "to suffer with," took on a deeper significance when one lived and worked among those on the margins of society. In his courses Don engaged students to think about how displacement brought them closer to understanding a God who is with us. This act of service to others was

---

8   Seminars are one-credit courses that address a social issue and include an immersion of typically one week, with classroom preparation before and after the immersion.

9   Joseph Komonchak, "The Local Realization of the Church," in *The Reception of Vatican II* (Washington, DC: CUA Press, 1987), 81.

10 Henri J. M. Nouwen, Donald P. McNeill, and Douglas A. Morrison, *Compassion: A Reflection on the Christian Life* (New York: Image Books Doubleday, 1982), 25.

an essential part of being church, a ministry that revealed God's love among us, especially among the suffering.

Developing relationships with people on the margins of society is an essential dimension of reading the signs of the times. The view from the margins is different from that from a privileged, safe place where many students find themselves; on the margins, people are excluded from many of the benefits of society. In recent years, the Summer Service Learning Program (SSLP) changed its course name to Kinship on the Margins to emphasize the importance of going to the margins. The course develops a theology of kinship, starting with Fr. Greg Boyle's *Tattoos on the Heart*, that invites students to develop relationships of solidarity with people who are marginalized due to social issues such as poverty, discrimination, mental illness, or disabilities. Students serve for eight weeks in a poor or underserved community and write reflections twice a week on the experience and the course readings. When they return to campus, groups of eight students meet with a facilitator a few times to further understand the signs of the times through the perspective of being on the margins. The SSLP team views this as a foundational course in lay formation that has a great impact on students' undergraduate experiences, especially since students participate much earlier than when the program first began. After the SSLP, students are invited to grow in their engagement with current social issues through other CSC programs and courses.

Another way that staff and faculty at the CSC respond to the signs of the times today is by developing courses and seminars based on the pressing needs of our time. For instance, fall and spring break seminars focus on going to places where students can learn about racial discrimination, human trafficking, women in poverty, incarceration, treatment of undocumented workers, border issues, environmental sustainability, gangs, child abuse, and many other pertinent issues. In the spring of 2016, the CSC seminars team developed a spring break course titled the Realities of Race in the

21st Century. Students traveled to Ferguson and Columbia, Missouri (home of Mizzou), and Chicago to learn firsthand about the recent experiences of racial discrimination and violence. Melissa Marley Bonnichsen, director of social concerns seminars, shared how seminar topics are chosen intentionally based upon a rubric that gauges the relevancy of the topic, how the topic reflects the needs of the most vulnerable in our society, and the level of interest shown by students and the center. She sees the work of the seminars as directly related to Vatican II's call for the church to be active participants in society. The seminar on race exemplifies the way in which seminars are chosen and conducted today at the CSC.

When seminars thoughtfully prepare students to reflect upon contemporary issues, students gain a greater understanding of the complexity of the issues and feel compelled to act upon them. While students who participated in the seminar on race came from varying levels of knowledge and experience, Bonnichsen commented that all students, regardless of their background, left with a deep understanding of the issues and a compelling call to action. Because of the seminar, students created action plans, gained an ability to converse about complex issues, helped to raise awareness on campus, and developed leadership skills. Upon hearing about the seminar, other students and faculty on campus have approached the seminars team to talk about other ways to get involved at the CSC.[11] Responding to the signs of the times proves to be an effective method to reach students, faculty, and community partners.

While the actual experience of immersion lays the groundwork to understand the signs of the times, Don understood that reflection and understanding are equally as important. When students returned from an immersion course such as the Urban Plunge, a spring break seminar, or a summer service project, Don asked them to think

---

11 Melissa Marley Bonnichsen, interview, May 2016.

deeply and critically about what they experienced. Whether in informal conversations, theology courses, or service experiences, Don was
constantly asking questions about the meaning and implications of
what students experienced. How did their experience make them feel?
What would they do because of it? What was stirred in their hearts,
and how would it lead them to action? How have they come to know
God in new and important ways? How does their faith call them to
leadership roles? These questions deepened students' understanding
and encouraged them to be involved in efforts for social change.
The center invites students into the practice of prayerfully pausing to
integrate life experiences meaningfully and purposefully into the next
stage of one's life. The many diverse programs of the CSC incorporate
faith-based reflection in one way or another into their coursework.
Programs such as the Urban Plunge, domestic and international
summer service programs, fall and spring break seminars, the discernment class, and others draw upon journaling and shared reflection as
integral parts of the coursework.

Reading about, and responding to, the signs of the times is both
challenging and exciting. It is critical in this process to include the
perspective from the margins of society and to engage community
partners as educators. At the center, we have found that strong
classroom preparation, immersions that displace students and invite
them into relationships, and personal and group reflection prove to
cultivate students' ability to respond to the pressing needs of our time.

THE LAITY

Don believed that lay formation was essential to building an active
church equipped to engage with the world. By persistently inviting
laypeople to be active in church and community, Don enacted the
inclusiveness espoused by Vatican II: "These faithful (the laity) are

by baptism made one body with Christ and are constituted among the People of God; they are in their own way made sharers in the priestly, prophetical, and kingly functions of Christ: and they carry out for their own part the mission of the whole Christian people in the Church and in the world."[12] In this spirit of inclusion, Vatican II impelled Don to live the Gospel in modern times viewed specifically through the lens of a preferential option for the poor. He made it a practice to invite the marginalized to the table and to ensure that as many people as possible were included in some way both during the liturgy and in his work at the CSC. He reached out to people of color and women, mentoring them and encouraging them to take leadership positions in the church and other areas. Whether as a friend, pastor, or teacher, Don acted upon the idea expressed in *Gaudium et Spes* that "enlightened by Christian wisdom and giving close attention to the teaching authority of the Church, let the layman take on his own distinctive role."[13] Through liturgical participation, a spirit of inclusion, and lay formation, Don empowered laypeople to find their distinctive roles.

Liturgical celebrations represented a unique opportunity for Don to express his multiple roles as priest, educator, and director of the CSC. Don saw the celebration of the Eucharist as intimately connected to his commitment to create a more just world; it simultaneously sustained him and acted as a vehicle to unify with others in the church working toward justice. Many students experienced the celebration of the Eucharist with Don as enlivening, catching the fire of the Spirit as reflected in *Sacrosanctum Concilium, The Constitution on Sacred Liturgy*:

> the renewal in the Eucharist of the covenant between the Lord and man draws the faithful into the compelling love of Christ and sets them on fire. From the liturgy,

12 *Lumen Gentium*, 31.
13 *Gaudium et Spes*, 43.

> therefore, and especially from the Eucharist, as
> from a font, grace is poured forth upon us; and the
> sanctification of men in Christ and the glorification
> of God, to which all other activities of the Church are
> directed as toward their end, is achieved in the most
> efficacious possible way.[14]

The Eucharist united the world in all of its diversity, especially with the vulnerable, and prepared Don and his students to better serve them.

Embracing the spirit of the liturgical reforms of Vatican II, Don invited students to participate in preaching, stand around the altar during the consecration, act as Eucharistic ministers, or say a closing prayer. In the 1970s and 1980s the chapels in residence halls were open spaces with little furniture where students typically sat on the floor. The chapels were welcoming and familial, like gathering as a family to celebrate a special meal. Don embraced the local culture in liturgy, whether with college students, professionals, informal gatherings, or Latino communities, inviting the use of music, participatory homilies, and cultural customs, artwork, and symbols to enhance the meaning and participation of those gathered. Whenever Don planned prayer or liturgy, he sought input, advice, and leadership from others to ensure that all voices were heard and that the prayer was as rich and relevant to those gathered as possible, thus representing the signs of the times as well as the diversity of all those gathered together.

It is impossible to discuss Don's commitment to inclusion and lay formation without highlighting his deep regard for women. One of his life's passions was encouraging the development of women's leadership in the church and the world. Vatican II fueled this passion in him. *The Church in the Modern World* states, "With respect to the fundamental rights of the person, every type of discrimination,

---

14   *Sacrosanctum Concilium*, 10.

whether social or cultural, whether based on sex, race, color, social condition, language, or religion, is to be overcome and eradicated as contrary to God's intent" (no. 29). Don lived out this belief that all people have equal rights and envisioned a church with equal opportunities, especially for women. In his professional, pastoral, and personal life, Don surrounded himself with women and relied on their feedback and advice when he made decisions. During high Masses at the Basilica, as a sign of solidarity with women he remained with the laity in the church pews rather than standing at the altar with dozens of men. He participated in Notre Dame's Committee to Ordain Women in the 1980s and 1990s and invited women to preach at Mass with him. Don worked closely with women in their own personal and professional development and encouraged them to take on positions of leadership, both on campus as undergraduates and after graduation.

Inspired by liberation theology, the influence of Fr. Virgil Elizondo, and his time in Chile, Don developed strong ties to Latino culture and spirituality. Whenever he celebrated Mass, Don wore his Chilean stole as a symbol of his desire to be in solidarity with the Latino community. At the CSC, he supported local Latino agencies in South Bend, celebrated Mass in Spanish for students, and hosted cultural events and Latin dancing at the center (he was not afraid of the dance floor!). After retiring from his position as executive director at the CSC, Don made it a priority to serve as a parish priest at St. Ann's, a Latino parish and school in Pilsen, located on the southwest side of Chicago. During this time, he immersed himself in the lives of his parishioners and their struggles related to immigration, poverty, and gangs. His love for Latino spirituality grew, as did his passion to increase vocations for Latino men and women. To this day, Don still speaks fondly of his many friendships with parish families, with whom he remains in close contact. While he was in Pilsen, he established the Metropolitan Chicago Initiative of the Institute for Latino Studies at the University of Notre Dame, which offered resources to students and faculty to undergo research in the local Pilsen community. By creating a bridge between the Institute for Latino Studies and the Chicago Latino community, Don supported efforts to accentuate the history and presence of Latino leaders and community organizers in society and in the church. In this same spirit, the CSC continues to embrace the Latino community through its many programs and partnership with the Institute for Latino Studies.

Don realized that he enjoyed many privileges as a white male member of the clergy. This awareness created a humility in him that invited others in. He gathered as many people as he could to come together; he was a bridge builder, a connector. He collaborated with other members of the Holy Cross Congregation and laypeople to create the Holy Cross Associates, a postgraduate service program that was another sign of his quest to incorporate the laity more fully into the life of the church and the Holy Cross order (as discussed in chapters 6, 7, and 8). Don was full of dreams and ideas for the future and had a unique charism that allowed others to come along for the ride and to engage in the building of that vision, whether on campus, in South Bend, in Chile, or in the Pilsen neighborhood of Chicago. Some may say that he allowed for too much input, perhaps a weakness that delayed decisions at times, but it didn't prevent him from taking real steps and action. Many of his dreams eventually became a reality but never without input from a diverse group of laypeople.

Don used his privilege to facilitate ways for students and the campus community to meet people whom they would not necessarily meet on their own, such as when he invited Henri Nouwen to come to campus with members of the L'Arche community or Marjorie Tuite to give workshops on power relationships. Don empowered students by challenging them again and again to try something totally new and out of their comfort zone and by connecting them with resources and leaders. In other words, Don often used his power and influence to empower others. Empowerment of the laity continues at the CSC through opportunities for leadership and growth as seminar leaders, in the Catholic Social Tradition minor, and in the discernment course Don began years ago. Fortunately, the role of women and Latinos in society is at a very different place than thirty years ago, but their roles in the church have yet to progress in the ways that Don and others hoped. Full participation in the church remains to be realized.

Mike Hebbeler, director of discernment and advocacy, continues the tradition of lay formation by teaching discernment seminars each year for seniors. He offers insights on the importance of reflection for students:

> The Discernment Seminar is designed to guide senior-level students in an exploration of their respective vocations through reflective practices and authentic conversation. Many fears and anxieties abound as soon-to-be graduates work through the pressures and expectations regarding future employment. They feel the tension between the culture's correlation of success with prestigious titles and monetary gain, and the Gospel's call to surrender and agapic love. The seminar provides a space for these students to voice these fears and accompany one another as they seek to discover God's will for their lives.[15]

Through these classes, students develop an aptitude for discernment, pausing to reflect and critically consider how to follow God's will in their unique calling and vocation.

A student in the Discernment Seminar shares about the learned value of reflection in her life: "The class . . . allowed me to explore my vocation more deeply and to understand, or begin to work

---

15   Mike Hebbeler, Center for Social Concerns Report, 2015.

to understand, both what I was being called to do in the present moment and in the future . . . I no longer view vocation solely as what job or career that I will pursue in the future. Rather, I see vocation as the journey in my life."[16] The CSC creates the space for students to step back from the busyness of college life to reflect on discerning their vocation, moving away from a focus on a career to a way of life, a skill that will serve them for the remainder of their lives.

Through his work at the CSC, Don lived out his vision to have a more inclusive church that empowered laity through spiritual, emotional, and intellectual formation and reflection. By focusing on lay formation of undergraduates, Latinos, and women, Don enlivened the spirit of Vatican II that beckons all of humanity to participate more fully in the life of the church.

ADVOCACY FOR JUSTICE

Inevitably, the consequence of responding to the signs of the times coupled with lay formation leads to action for justice. *Gaudium et Spes* affirms the church's embrace of the world and the need to act for justice: "The Church recognizes that worthy elements are found in today's social movements, especially an evolution toward unity, a process of wholesome socialization and of association in civic and economic realms."[17] Continuing in the spirit of Vatican II, the Synod of Bishops produced the 1971 document *Justice in the World*, which states that "action on behalf of justice and participation in the trans-formation of the world fully appear to us as a constitutive dimension of the preaching of the Gospel."[18] In the early days of the Center for Experiential Learning and the Center for Social Concerns, students

---

16   Jaclyn Paul, quoted in Center for Social Concerns Report, 2015. Permission received June 2, 2016.

17   *Gaudium et Spes*, 42.

18   Synod of Bishops, *Justice in the World* (1971), 6.

found great inspiration in these documents and sought to live a life that integrated faith with action for justice to transform the world.

Don aspired to set the world on fire by educating and equipping students to be agents for change in church and in society. By providing an education at the CSC rooted in Gospel values and prayer that engaged students with the signs of the times, Don promoted advocacy for justice. *Gaudium et Spes* proclaims that all of humanity participates in the joy and suffering of each other and calls us to be responsible to each other.[19] Through CSC programs and seminars, students formed relationships with their brothers and sisters in Christ, especially among the marginalized, and because of those relationships were called to action and advocacy.

With attention to both the local community and communities across the globe, Don had a special relationship with the people of Chile and shared that relationship with students by inviting them to take the Seminar on Poverty and Development while studying in the semester-abroad program in Chile. Christine Raslavsky is one of many students who, when confronted by poverty, asked questions about herself and the United States and responded to the call to opt for the poor:

> The option for the poor asks everyone to realize the
> plight of those who struggle to survive, and to put the
> needs of these most vulnerable members of society
> ahead of individual Selfish interests . . . We need to
> ask "why?" Why are people starving around the world?
> How can the United States, the richest nation in the
> world, allow its people to live in poverty, to be homeless
> in the "land of opportunity," to lack good education
> and adequate health care and to starve to death? . . .

---

19 *Gaudium et Spes*, 1, 55.

As one of the elite—the fed, the clothed, the sheltered,
the educated—what are my responsibilities as I step out
into this unjust world society and try to make my way?[20]

Courses and programs at the CSC regularly encourage students to
ask why, as they become aware of disparities in economics, education,
health care, and opportunities for human flourishing. The act of
questioning is one of the first steps toward becoming an advocate
for justice. As Christine continued to reflect on her responsibilities,
she eventually cofounded Maggie's Place, a home for expectant and
young mothers in Phoenix, Arizona.

In his course Theology and Social Ministry, Don was at his
best when he worked with small groups of student activists. Don
required students in his courses to take on projects that addressed
issues of justice at the university. Students met with the president of
the university and other leaders to advocate for change. Initiatives
included taking leftover food from the dining hall to a local farmer
for pig feed, involving the university in neighborhood improvement
just south of campus, and encouraging the monitoring of factories
where university products were made to ensure workers' rights. Today,
students advocate on a range of issues, such as trying to convince the
student body to refrain from using trays in the dining hall to prevent
food waste, creating an organization to support undocumented
students on campus and locally, or silently protesting for a higher
living wage for campus workers. Students, faculty, and staff continue
to speak out about workers' rights in the factories where university
products are made in response to the proposed new policy that would
allow university products to be made in China.

The courses and programs that Don started continue to
transform students as the student involvement and the size of the

---

20   Christine Raslavsky, Seminar on Poverty and Development in Chile, 1995. Permission received
    August 14, 2016.

center staff increase. For example, issues of justice related to migrant farm workers are still being explored by students who participate in the Immokalee Migrant Worker Seminar each spring. Melody Gonzales, a student in the seminar, reflected on her family history of migrant farming and her participation in the class:

> One morning we headed to the parking lot where workers gather to look for work at 4 am. We were able to get on a bus to go pick tomatoes at Pacific, one of the largest tomato companies. As we were out in the fields, under 90-degree weather and humidity, I thought about my father and his family. I observed the faces around me, mostly young men from southern Mexico and Guatemala, some from Haiti. All were working as fast as they could, sweat dripping from their faces.[21]

After working in the fields, the students visited the office of the Coalition of Immokalee Workers and learned about the Taco Bell boycott. Melody observed, "This awakened a movement across the entire country where consumers, me included, saw ourselves also in that supply chain and our responsibility to hold companies accountable for profiting from sub poverty wages."[22] This insight led Melody to organize students at Notre Dame. She educated students about unjust wages and worked to have Taco Bell removed from campus. The campaign, both on campus and nationally, succeeded as companies agreed to pay more for tomatoes in order to increase farm worker wages.

Building on Don's vision, the faculty and staff of the center hope that participation in the seminars, summer experiences, and community engagement courses leads to further involvement,

---

21   Melody Gonzalez, service send-off talk, University of Notre Dame, May 2016.
22   Ibid.

finding one's passion, and, ultimately, social action. Christine discovered her passion for young mothers and dedicated herself to creating the mission Maggie's Place. Melody's example points to ways that students bring the issues from the seminars back to campus to educate the wider student body. She, too, has gone on to become a community organizer, working on behalf of workers' rights. These are just two examples of countless students who became advocates for change in society, in part because of the influence of CSC programs. We hope that students continue to build upon their formation in faith and justice and to use these skills as they discern their career paths and lifestyles beyond the college years to become advocates for social justice.

At the age of eighty, Don continues to keep abreast of current events and to think about his call to be countercultural. While his physical health prevents him from getting out and about much, he wonders, "Should I eat at this restaurant that is populated only with white people? Should I stand on the altar to be unified with my Holy Cross brothers or sit with the congregation? How do I accept my own physical pain and suffering as a way to be in solidarity with those who have endured torture?" Don's example still inspires us to ask difficult questions about small and large decisions in our lives.

Similar questions remain at the forefront of the work of the center. For instance, how ought we individually and collectively respond to the economic inequalities and lack of opportunity for all people? How ought we respond to the challenges of a diverse student body, including religion, race, and sexual orientation? The university that once drew mostly middle-class students now draws more students from very privileged backgrounds as well as students who have high financial need. A new challenge is to create an environment where all are welcome and have their needs met. In what ways can we facilitate courses and processes so that students from all points along the economic spectrum learn from each other as they participate in community engagement? The list of questions and challenges is endless. The center strives to live out the mission of the university, "where learning becomes service to justice." As the university becomes more corporate and diverse, this mission becomes increasingly challenging.

The Center for Social Concerns' call to respond to the vision and challenges of Vatican II persists. Today's social issues demand inquiry and boldness as much as they did fifty years ago. Inclusion and empowerment of the laity, particularly those who live on the margins of society, remain ongoing needs. In the past three decades, the Center for Social Concerns addressed many of the emerging social issues and faithfully grounded its education for justice in Catholic social thought, but there is still much work to be done. The vision of its founders and challenges of the day spur us to join with colleagues and students in further study and action. How will we live out this courageous vision?

Don is well known for his expression of *"Gracias"* at the end of Mass or with a gathering of friends. He reminds us to be grateful for the opportunities to build relationships with people on the margins, to give thanks for gathering together to celebrate the Eucharist, and to appreciate the gift of life. We express *Gracias* to Don for his vision to create the Center for Social Concerns so that it might bring about justice, love goodness, and walk humbly with our God. Indeed, Don modeled these values with his life. Thanks to him, education based on the founding principles of reading the signs of the times, empowering the laity, and promoting advocacy for justice continues to thrive in the center's fourth decade.

CHAPTER 2

Vatican II and Lay Formation:
The Early Years of the Community for
the International Lay Apostolate (CILA)

Maureen R. O'Brien

*C*ILA's main goal is to work for justice in the world by serving, learning, celebrating, and sharing with one another and a multiple of people contacted through a variety of activities. CILA's challenge is to discover how these experiences are related to the ongoing tradition of Christianity and its goals of love of neighbor, and love of God.[23]

CILA is a group of students, who with faculty and administration, come together out of a common need to learn of others who are brothers [and sisters], but are deprived. It is an attempt to do something for them, and also to do something for us . . . However, this is not a blaring holy-roller type of feeling. Rather it is a strong, silent enthusiasm that does its work and then lets those affected judge the results themselves. It is the

---

23 "CILA: Council for the International Lay Apostolate" (brochure, n.d.), 3.

coming together of these people to discuss concerns or experiences, and attempts to further them. Finally, it is a community that besides trying to help our neighbors, are trying to open up to the hardest of all places to share and love—one's own home.[24]

At the University of Notre Dame, an organization called the Council for the International Lay Apostolate (CILA) was formed in 1960–1961. Over the following two decades, it provided hundreds of students at Notre Dame and Saint Mary's College a unique opportunity for growth in faith as integrally connected with service and justice. I was fortunate to be part of CILA during the mid- to late 1970s. I was drawn to join it in my first weeks as a Notre Dame freshman with a vague desire to "do service," and CILA became my primary context for growth in belonging, leadership, and an educated sense of the faith that does justice. I participated regularly in CILA events, completed a summer CILA service project in Boston, served as an officer for spiritual formation, and took several courses that developed from CILA initiatives. Because of CILA, I look back at those years as the most formative—and transformative—of my life. A student of theology, I gained practice and conviction through CILA to shape my theological approach in a practical and pastoral mode: engaging in experience, reflecting upon it in disciplined dialogue with Christian tradition, and then acting for the sake of a more just and peaceful world.

Nothing begins in a vacuum. CILA emerged on a particular college campus in a particular era, shaped by major renewals in the Catholic Church and important shifts in society. The church's renewed vision called all its members to participate in discipleship in the modern world, and CILA helped to incarnate this vision in ways

---

24 Mike Maguire, "CILA Is . . .," course paper, Religion and Human Development 331 (September 17, 1973), 3.

suited to the dreams, aspirations, and needs of college students at that time. Here, I hope to illuminate the distinctive aspects of CILA's formation of young Catholic laity—ND and SMC students—as evident during the organization's first two decades. To set the scene, I will first summarize the major factors in the church that influenced the development of CILA, then proceed to an overview of its first twenty years. Finally, I will bring the voices of students more fully into dialogue with these events to show some important ways in which CILA sponsored their formation as reflective and prayerful laity, called into the church's mission of action for service and justice in the world.

Numerous developments in the twentieth-century Catholic Church can be seen as contributing to the energies on the Notre Dame campus before and during the beginnings of CILA. Through the 1960s, these renewals converged in the Second Vatican Council and continued to nourish the organization's efforts.

First, the numerous church documents comprising Catholic social teaching are typically dated to the promulgation by Pope Leo XIII of *Rerum Novarum* in 1891. Throughout the 1900s, popes, synods, and episcopal conferences built a significant body of work in which they brought insights from theological, economic, and social analysis to the issues of their day. Treating topics such as workers' rights, exploitation of the poor, unjust aspects of capitalism and communism, racism, war and violence, and sinful institutional structures, they advocated for social justice and called upon all people of good will to join in this effort.

In CILA's early years, references to two key encyclicals of Pope John XXIII—*Mater et Magistra* (*Christianity and Social Progress*, 1961) and *Pacem in Terris* (*Peace on Earth*, 1963)—showed the group's engagement with social teaching. An article by two CILA members in *The Scholastic* magazine, for example, cited these as the basis for its work "to help its members understand some of the complexities of this world, some of their responsibilities, and some of their opportunities."[25] *Mater et Magistra*, written amid the post–World War II emergence of new nations, called for international attention to human rights, criticized growing economic disparities between wealthy and poor nations, affirmed the potential of science and technology to benefit all humankind, and urged subsidiarity as a guiding principle for development. *Pacem in Terris* affirmed basic human dignity and the rights and duties of citizens and nations alike; advocated for an end to the arms race, especially calling for nuclear disarmament; affirmed the dignity of women and their growing role in society; and called for all to work toward the common good.

Documents of Vatican Council II (1962–1965) further developed aspects of Catholic social teaching relevant to CILA's early identity. Notable in this regard is *Gaudium et Spes* (*Pastoral Constitution on the Church in the Modern World*, 1965). It outlined a theological anthropology emphasizing dignity and universal human community, affirmed the fundamental role of family as cornerstone of society, and addressed respect for cultural values and economic justice and the need to foster peace. It called for the church to recognize its place in the world as one of fundamental service and solidarity with all people: "The joys and the hopes, the griefs and the anxieties of the [people] of this age, especially those who are poor or in any way afflicted, these are the joys and hopes, the griefs and anxieties of the followers of Christ. Indeed, nothing genuinely human fails to raise an echo in their hearts."[26]

As is often observed, Pope John XXIII, and the council whose vision he shaped, adopted a notably hopeful tone. While cognizant of the challenges of the times, they pointed to promising developments in numerous realms of human life and looked with optimism into the future. The early 1960s were also a time of idealism and

---

25 Peter Collins and Gary Shaffer, "CILA," *The Scholastic* (October 2, 1964): 20.
26 *Gaudium et Spes*, 1.

commitments to service for young people in the United States. It is fair to say that this optimism helped inspire the founders of CILA and direct its early years of growth.

Second, the theology and practice of mission by religious orders—notably, Maryknoll and Holy Cross—infused the development of CILA from its beginnings and were themselves transformed during the early CILA years by new currents of thinking at Vatican II.

Work in "the missions" was important for a number of American religious orders in the twentieth century, as they sought to carry the Gospel to all corners of the world. Bringing the call to Christian conversion as well as material assistance through education, medicine, and social services, these missionary orders established themselves in Africa, Asia, and Latin America. With the council, however, both theology and practice of mission underwent decisive changes. The decree *Ad Gentes* (*On the Mission Activity of the Church*, 1965) proclaimed, "The pilgrim Church is missionary by her very nature, since it is from the mission of the Son and the mission of the Holy Spirit that she draws her origin, in accordance with the decree of God the Father."[27] The church as mission is rooted in the mission of the Trinity. Vatican II conceived of church as the sacrament of Christ's salvation in the world, rather than standing apart from it. Thus, all its members were sent forth on "mission," with the singular rather than plural use of the term connoting the unity of the common call.

Further, respect for human dignity—with emphasis on mutuality and solidarity—and for the cultures encountered in mission was reinforced by Catholic social teaching and the work of the council. The cultural paternalism that frequently characterized missionary work in previous centuries was addressed with attention to mutuality of relationships and the imperative to bring the Gospel alive within the richness of local cultures. "Let the young church keep up an

---

27 *Ad Gentes*, 2.

intimate communion with the whole Church, whose tradition they should link to their own culture, in order to increase, by a certain mutual exchange of forces, the life of the Mystical Body."[28] Those on mission were encouraged to be open to learning and growth through those they encountered.

By the middle of the twentieth century, laypeople were being invited into this missionary work as collaborators with priests and vowed religious.[29] As CILA took shape in the early 1960s, its student members were guided into their initial projects through the international networks of these experienced people, amid the exciting and sometimes tumultuous re-examination of their own mission purposes.

Third, perhaps the most significant impetus for the growth of CILA was the creative ferment of the twentieth century that inspired Catholic laity to incarnate their faith in all areas and circumstances of their lives. While Vatican II is often credited with this emphasis, it was building over previous decades. Notably, numerous forms of "Catholic Action" had developed, encouraged by the exhortations of popes such as Pius XI in *Quadragesimo Anno*: Catholic Action laity are "imbue[d] with Catholic principles and train[ed] for carrying on an apostolate under the leadership and teaching guidance of the Church."[30] With the lofty aim of reconstructing the social order according to the values of Christ and His church, many lay associations sprang up—societies and sodalities, movements and leagues—some more closely connected to the hierarchy than others. Laymen and laywomen sought as well to contribute in their everyday spheres of family, workplace, local church, and community. The term "lay apostolate" became common in this period, connoting both the collective and individual efforts of the laity to fulfill their vocations. International congresses on the lay apostolate were held in

---

28 Ibid., 19.
29 *Ad Gentes'* chapter III, "Missionaries," refers to laity, along with priests and religious, as missionaries.
30 *Quadragesimo Anno*, 96.

midcentury, and theologians provided the contours for a reconceiving of the laity's place in the church.

Drawing on this heritage, Vatican II offered a vital new articulation of the theological foundations for the laity's exercise of their calling. The Apostolic Constitution on the Church, *Lumen Gentium* (1964), located the nature and mission of the church foremost within the mystery of the dynamic life and communion of the Trinity, rather than in its hierarchical structures. As People of God, all "[t] he baptized, by regeneration and the anointing of the Holy Spirit, are consecrated as a spiritual house and a holy priesthood, in order that through all those works which are those of the Christian [person] they may offer spiritual sacrifices and proclaim the power of Him who has called them out of darkness into His marvelous light."[31] The council fathers affirmed that there is a universal call to holiness, which all pursue on their common pilgrimage.

Within this single vocation, laity were called to exercise a specific role as "leaven" in society, working for the "sanctification of the world from within."[32] Vatican II devoted a later document, *Apostolicam Actuousitatem*, to further description of this "lay apostolate." Once again, the bishops of the council advocated the engagement of laypeople in their everyday exercise of faith, hope, and charity amid "temporal" responsibilities of family, work, and civic life. Yet their essential relationality as people of God and Body of Christ also would lead them into informal and formal modes of "group apostolate," with mutual support as well as effectiveness heightened through such gathering and releasing of common energies.[33] CILA can certainly be viewed as a vibrant expression of this group apostolate, with the strongly campus-centered nature of Notre Dame and Saint Mary's providing ample opportunities for planning and enacting common endeavors. As CILA

---

31 *Lumen Gentium*, 10.
32 Ibid., 31.
33 *Apostolicam Actuousitatem* (*Decree on the Apostolate of the Laity*, 1965), 18.

students, we could walk to Bulla Shed for "sharing sessions" at 10:00 p.m. on Wednesdays and crowd into the chairperson's dorm room for late-night officers' meetings. Big ideas and practical organizational details, dreams, and struggles alike could be engaged regularly through face-to-face dialogue (complete with a lot of laughter).

Fourth, while space does not permit extensive treatment of liturgical and scriptural renewals, their developments in the nineteenth and twentieth centuries and the impetus of Vatican II also would affect CILA as a lay student organization. The dramatic changes in Catholic worship catalyzed by the council built upon decades of historical research and liturgical experimentation and sought to promote the active participation of the entire worshipping assembly.[34] The liturgical renewal included exploration of the integral links between worship, prayer, and action for justice. Further, the renewal movements and the council brought greater emphasis on the living power of God's Word in scripture and the encouragement of Catholics to study and pray with the Bible. These dynamic currents had important effects on college campuses as students were invited into communities where faith and action were deemed equally essential and closely connected. The liturgically rich environment of ND and SMC brought abundant opportunities, through CILA and many other initiatives, for students to deepen their experience of shared prayer and scriptural immersion, along with finding in the Eucharist a deep wellspring of nourishment for the work of service and justice. I still remember how our gathering around an outdoor altar for Mass on weekend retreats changed the meaning of liturgy for me. I experienced a new sense of the Eucharist as a joyous community celebration and one in which I had an integral role. I later expanded that role by becoming a coordinator for our liturgies, singing with the music ministers, and offering reflections on scripture readings.

---

34   *Sacrosanctum Concilium* (*Constitution on the Sacred Liturgy,* 1963), 11.

Liturgy as the work of God's people became the source for any "good works" I hoped to do through CILA service projects and studies.

With these themes and experiences in mind, I will now turn to an overview of CILA's first two decades. Short histories of CILA have typically outlined several phases over these years, after which CILA's work became part of the new Center for Social Concerns in the early 1980s. I will identify two major stages, roughly corresponding to the 1960s (during the group's establishment and initial growth) and the 1970s (with some decline, followed by significant reorganization and growth).

The archival materials on CILA's first stage provide a founding story: a group of Notre Dame and Saint Mary's students began to gather at Old College with Larry Murphy, MM, in 1960, to discuss "the relationship between traditional Catholic social teaching and personal Christian commitment."[35] Discussion soon led to active responses, and the group initiated some local community service during that school year. However, in the fall of 1961 its primary emphasis became the "international lay apostolate," as evident in the group's name. With the aid of Murphy and Ernest Bartell, C.S.C., in locating viable sites, students began to plan international service projects. In 1962, CILA sent eighteen to twenty students to three projects, one in Peru and two in Mexico. Beginning in 1966, project sites were located in the United States as well as Latin America. By 1968, the number of students participating in projects had doubled to forty.

CILA's constitution showed how the founding members sought to position their identity within the dimensions articulated in

---

35 Mike Glockner, "The Council for the International Lay Apostolate: A Model for a Spirituality of Social Action," course paper, Theology of Social Ministry, Theology 548 (spring semester, 1977), 3. Other information in this paragraph comes from Glockner. He also notes that while CILA was initially formalized as a Notre Dame group and thus restricted to men (pre-coeducation at the university), in 1966 it merged with the Saint Mary's College Columbian Project and was thereafter composed of both men and women.

the first part of this essay. While explicitly claiming not to be a Catholic Action group, as lay students they highlighted "the right and responsibility of the [layperson] to take an active part in the life and work of the Church in the world."[36] They desired collaboration with clergy in their initiatives while acknowledging a distinct status as laypeople. Their purpose was threefold: deepening the Catholic identity and commitment of members, serving the ND-SMC students and community, and engaging in forms of local and international service. Prospective members were to apply to the CILA board.

The interwoven priorities inherent in CILA's purpose were evident in the projects from the beginning. Students served on site by accomplishing specific tasks; for the international sites, these typically involved construction of housing and other facilities to aid poor people. But such activities were combined with theological and social analysis, reflection, and dialogue that made them educational and formative of the participants as Catholic and lay. Each project group received an orientation to the culture they would be entering, engaging in readings and discussions with one another and with faculty resource people prior to departure. They attended events that deepened their knowledge of the local context. They were encouraged throughout to place themselves in solidarity with the poor among whom they were guests. And in accord with their resolve to serve the ND-SMC students and community, they prepared reports on their experiences and gave on-campus presentations during the school year. For several years, CILA members contributed vivid articles and photos from their summer projects for *The Scholastic*.

The transition to CILA's second stage began in the late 1960s and early 1970s. CILA underwent a period of decline in its international summer projects, as the rise in oil prices and greater political instability in Latin America—along with broader American disillusionment

---

36   *CILA Constitution* (n.d.), 1.

with their government and civil turmoil—led to problems in financing the projects and deterred student participation.[37] There was also questioning of the efficacy of projects and their educational quality. The ensuing "soul-searching" led to more thorough project organization and supervision through Notre Dame faculty and advisors. The educational impact of the experiences was also considerably deepened through the design of accompanying credit courses—a feature that would become a signature of CILA and, later, related initiatives at the university. For example, the establishment of the Religion and Human Development course in 1973 allowed for "a more sophisticated preparation for the summer projects and for more intensive and fruitful evaluations of the experiences."[38] Several students who enrolled in the 1974 course Religion and World Injustice (cotaught by Hubert Horan and Don McNeill, C.S.C.) helped to establish new organizations such as the World Hunger Coalition and the Latin American Program for Experiential Learning (LAPEL), through which students could spend an academic year working with members of the congregation of the Holy Cross in Chile or Peru, eventually earning academic credit.[39]

CILA was further reconceived and re-energized in the 1970s as students and faculty advisors developed their vision for a group that retained the original commitments to service, personal growth in Catholic identity, and building campus awareness but did so through a more local and US focus as well as increased integration of educational components. Summer projects were sponsored in a number of US cities. CILA developed more community service projects in South Bend and combined these with courses such as Don McNeill's Theology and Community Service, in which students visited local nursing homes and brought their experiences into

---

37 Several sources provide this information, including Glockner, 4, and "CILA: Twenty Years, 1960–80" (paper, n.d.), 2.
38 Glockner, 4.
39 "CILA: Twenty Years," 5.

dialogue with sources in pastoral theology and spirituality. A later interdisciplinary course, the Unseen City, offered a team of faculty from political science (John Roos), economics (Tom Swartz), and theology (Don McNeill) departments who taught on urban issues.

These two courses were especially strong occasions for my own growth as a student and a Catholic Christian. In Theology and Community Service, we journaled after each nursing home visit in conjunction with the weekly assigned readings. I still have my journals and final case study. And I still marvel at the careful and caring comments that Don McNeill made in the margins of the journals and the extensive feedback he provided for my case study. I was learning to do theology grounded in experience—and, in particular, the experience of seeking solidarity with the elderly as "living human documents" worthy of respect on their own terms. Knowing I would be supported, I could take risks—not the kind that involve physical danger but risks to my comfortable assumptions about others and the need for my own humility and acceptance of them in order to enter relationship. In the Unseen City, I did a final project with two other students through which we researched, did interviews, and ultimately made a proposal for a freshman orientation segment on social concerns. Supported by our professors, we negotiated the necessary approvals and offered that program the following year. Furthermore, though I didn't know it, I was also being empowered for my future career as an academic. Don invited me to assist in the course during its second iteration, and we eventually coauthored a paper about it for competitive journal review and publication.

A key factor in strengthening CILA during this period was its partnership with the Catholic Committee on Urban Ministry (CCUM), an organization devoted to cultivating strong community organization and empowerment strategies for the urban poor. CCUM provided sites and resource people for CILA summer projects in the United States. And with CCUM assistance, CILA expanded its impact on the broader ND-SMC community through the short-term, intensive experience called Urban Plunge. In its first offering during the 1976 Christmas break, Urban Plunge attracted one hundred thirty participants to several cities, with students visiting community agencies, learning about the problems of cities, and engaging in reflection with church leaders, while also earning academic credit.[40]

By the mid- to late 1970s, CILA had a fully delineated structure of offices including chairperson, communications, community service, education, fundraising, social, spiritual formation, and summer projects. The 1976–1977 membership directory listed one hundred forty-eight members, along with faculty advisors for each office. Besides their community service and summer projects, members participated in numerous activities throughout the year: biweekly liturgies, regular reflection groups on campus or in faculty mentors' homes, weekends away for planning in fall and a retreat in the spring (retreat leaders included John Dunne, C.S.C., and Henri Nouwen), socials each semester, and a lakeside sending Mass for graduates in May.[41] In this period CILA changed the first word of its title from "council" to "community," indicating a sense of identity focused in relationality rather than official procedures and tasks.

As already noted, this growth and development coincided with a period of diminished idealism and social concern in American society as people became disillusioned by the Vietnam War, assassinations, the Kent State shootings, and the limited success of previous political and economic reforms. Mary Beckman, the 1974 CILA president who helped to galvanize the changes in CILA's second decade by leading its major reorganization, later reflected that CILA was countercultural in continuing its mission in this climate of widespread apathy: "In CILA, concern about injustice has broadened in scope, deepened in commitment, and strengthened in

---

40 Glockner, 6.
41 *CILA Handbook: The Community for the International Lay Apostolate*, 1978–79, 2–5.

models of effective action."[42] Glockner observed that "over a period of sixteen years the charismatic in CILA has become increasingly, and beneficially, professionalized,"[43] a necessary process to sustain its commitments as circumstances and attitudes changed. Don McNeill was instrumental in guiding the group and opening areas of institutional support at Notre Dame throughout these years. The establishment of the Center for Experiential Learning, according to McNeill's 1977 Annual Report, was "because CILA members saw the need for more coordination of their projects, educational workshops and retreats, training for various skills concerning their apostolates, and closer contact with support faculty."[44] In the 1980s, these and several other university initiatives would converge through McNeill's leadership in founding the Center for Social Concerns.

In reading CILA students' writings and recalling my own experience, it is undeniable that CILA was profoundly formative of us as laity. I've continued to feel the power of its influence on my professional, personal, and spiritual life dimensions for more than forty years. In this final part, I will describe two major ways that CILA served as a university-based incubator for the growth of young Catholic laity into the renewed sense of mission of the twentieth-century church.

First, CILA provided a living integration of experience in service and justice work with prayer, learning, critical analysis, and community formation. In this way it was deeply consonant with the vision of Catholic social teaching and the calling of all the baptized into full participation, as church, in God's desires for the world. It combined its key formative elements with emphasis on the life-changing nature of encounter and relationship with diverse others, especially the poor and oppressed. It invited members, most of whom

---

42   Mary Beckman, "Students and Social Change," *Connector* (April 1976): 1.
43   Glockner, 16.
44   Don McNeill, 1977 Annual Report, Center for Experiential Learning, 6–7.

would remain lay, into a holistic exercise of their apostolate through these experiences.

Immersion into service projects was at the heart of the CILA experience. Yet before, during, and after service, we were encouraged to move beyond simple initial desires to "do good" into a multifaceted practice of work, study, dialogue and reflection, prayer and community. During the first summer of CILA projects, for example, Tom Schlereth went to Peru, where, after working during the day, he participated in evening meetings with local university students, business leaders, church leaders, and others.[45] Citing *Mater et Magistra*, he wrote of his realization that for both himself and the poor in Peru, Christian faith is not confined to prayer and sacraments but requires action for justice—which is itself nurtured through rich liturgical experiences.[46] In the 1970s, Sue Olin worked during the days at a center in New Orleans focused on empowerment of the poor. In the evenings she read resources such as encyclicals, social analyses, and poverty reports and attended meetings focused on urban problems.[47] The New Orleans 1978 Project Report affirmed the five key dimensions of CILA summer projects as they were experienced by participants: Christian community, service and social action with supervision, experiential learning, simple lifestyle, and accountability to Notre Dame and Saint Mary's to report on their experiences.[48] In my own summer project experience in Boston, I came to know the power of conversation with my fellow CILA members and our priest mentors around the rectory dinner table. At the end of long, hot days working with urban children in a local daycare center or assisting a community organization in developing mailings and canvassing the neighborhood, we found ourselves making connections between faith, poverty, and the practical limitations of our efforts.

45 Tom Schlereth, "Summer Lay Apostolate: Peru," *The Scholastic* (September 28, 1962): 32–34.
46 Tom Schlereth, "Summer Lay Apostolate: Peru," *The Scholastic* (October 5, 1962): 34.
47 Sue Olin, "CILA Summer Project Report, May 29–July 29, 1978, New Orleans, LA" (n.d.), 7–8.
48 "Model CILA Summer Project, New Orleans, La., 1978" (n.d.), 1–4.

Catholic social thought and Vatican II, particularly in *Gaudium et Spes*, advocated respect for the essential dignity of the human person, the importance of viewing ourselves as one human family, and the need to honor people's cultures. Service projects, integrated with education, prayer, and reflection, were vital means for CILA members to recognize human connectedness and to be open to how encounters with others, especially the poor, could be occasions of God's grace. As expressed by member Tim Ready, while the tangible benefits to the poor from CILA service projects might be small, there was an important way that encounter with them helped to move students beyond their stereotypes:

> If understanding is a prerequisite to love, then it would certainly be reasonable for Christians interested in loving their neighbor to (1) understand the ways of life of other peoples through study, and ideally, to (2) encounter first-hand some of the grit of living experienced every day by those with less fortune than ourselves.
>
> This, then, is the aim of CILA: to attain an honest understanding of our neighbors in different cultural settings, so that we might realistically relate to them, thus enabling us to fulfill Christ's commandment of love.[49]

We in CILA understood service as necessarily connected with efforts to foster loving and authentic relationships, guided by the model of Jesus—and we learned firsthand of the messiness and mixed results of our efforts. On my Boston project, I was reduced to tears when a homeless and alcoholic man at Pine Street Inn shouted at me, ridiculing my efforts to befriend him as someone who could

---

49   Tim Ready, "CILA: It's [sic] Aims," in "CILA 1972 Summer Project Reports" (n.d.), 3.

never know what it meant to live in his situation. And, of course, he was right; I couldn't. Through encounters like this, I learned that trying to live like Jesus would bring pain and uncertainty and require sustained prayer and support.

On campus, while new and less experienced people like me might come to CILA attracted by its welcoming community and the desire to serve the "less fortunate," seasoned CILA members and officers continually sought to deepen and balance these motivations with other dimensions. As has been noted, regular liturgical celebrations and social events were important for our identity. Yet education was, for some, the paramount and most strongly formative dimension. In a sociology paper, Stephen Dane conducted interviews of CILA members and concluded that "older" (i.e., longer-term and more deeply committed) members recognized the value of education to explore the issues of global injustice, develop their Christian commitments, and thus be challenged both to growth in faith and action for social justice. "In fact, many experienced CILA members will claim that education of its members is the primary purpose of CILA, and that community service and community support are merely methods of achieving it."[50]

The impact of this integrated formation and participation could be profound and long-lasting. For me, it has shaped ever since my vision of how Christian discipleship is lived and nurtured in community. And indeed, this was part of CILA's intent, as articulated in a 1974 alumni newsletter: "We believe that CILA is much more than summer projects and four years in residence at Notre Dame or St. Mary's . . . To all of us, CILA is not a four-year involvement that ceases after graduation, but the beginning of a lifetime of dedication to Christian service."[51] CILA was indeed fostering the "universal

---

50   Stephen M. Dane, "CILA as a Medium for Growth," course paper for Culture and Society 228 (December 5, 1977), 5.
51   *CILA Alumni Newsletter* (July 1974): 1.

call to holiness" of Vatican II, as well as promoting the exercise by laypeople of their mission to transform the world in the sectors where they found themselves.

Second, CILA encouraged and expected that students with willingness and openness would be formed and transformed through a dynamic, tension-filled, and always self-articulated process.

According to *Lumen Gentium,* "all the faithful of Christ of whatever rank or status, are called to the fullness of the Christian life and to the perfection of charity."[52] This is at its heart a journey of conversion and growth into an ever-deepening practice of discipleship. In CILA, we as young Catholic laity found this journey challenging and fulfilling. We were invited to change and to extend the invitation to others as well. And we were continually invited to reflect on the persons we were becoming. As I grew and matured in CILA, I gained necessary realism relative to the lofty call to "the fullness of the Christian life and to the perfection of charity." At the same time, I learned that the challenge and invitation to pursue these must endure as a beacon of the Reign of God—a reign already in our midst through Jesus yet ever calling us forward.

However, such change was much more complex and sometimes painful in practice than in church documents. Student project reports and papers for coursework provide a rich trove of testimonials to tensions, paradoxes, and questions occasioned by CILA experiences. Some reflections resulted in partial appropriation, with dissonance and confusion. In 1968, Tony Ingraffea quoted a CILA member who regretted his failure to converse with an old peasant man who greeted him as the student hurried to finish his day's work on his project in Mexico.[53] A writer for the 1973 summer project in Clarksdale, Mississippi, admitted:

---

52 *Lumen Gentium,* 40.
53 Ingraffea, 30.

> I think most of us are driven by a sense of obligation:
> we should help, and this plugs at our consciences until
> we do. But does appeasement of conscience constitute
> adherence to the commandment "Love thy neighbor"?
> I doubt it. It is more neurosis than love—we help not
> because we really want to, but because we are literally
> driven to. We cannot live with ourselves if we don't.[54]

This writer also acknowledges that he and his project partners never vigorously engaged these questions together during the summer—yet they became deeply reliant on one another for support as they wrestled daily with both the difficulties of their work and the resulting unanswered questions.

For others, a central issue that fostered personal change became the way they regarded the people with whom they worked on projects, combined with awareness of the larger systemic issues raised by the disparity in their lifestyles. A member from a Mexico project described the juxtaposition of affluence with the poverty of the peasants and what he saw as the paradox of the Mexican poor's envy for the wealth of Americans—paradoxical, for him, in that the CILA students were closest to authentic "life" when among the poor and became more distant from life only when leaving them.[55] Such acknowledgment of the poor's greater "humanity" and closeness to Christ also were evident in the reflections of one of the 1973 St. Lucia project participants, quoted by author Joe Marino:

> [I]t's true . . . in an "underdeveloped" country—
> "humanity" and a similarity to Christ is more evident,
> much more so than here in the competitive business type
> world of the U.S. Those people reminded me of Christ,

---

54 "Clarksdale, Mississippi" (n.d.), 16.
55 Ingraffea, 32.

because Christ loved children so. I think that their
simplicity and their anti-hustleness affected us all.[56]

In the same paper, however, Marino quotes a participant who
noted that rapid industrialization would inevitably change these
people's lifestyle and pondered the economic and social consequences,
ultimately arguing for the right to self-determination of the St.
Lucian people. She further affirmed the solidarity that the students
experienced with the local people as a coparticipation in the Body of
Christ. Now back home, she experienced the call to fulfillment of her
vocation in continued commitment to the poor, seeing that God calls
us to "put to use both the mind and the natural resources which God
has given."[57]

As evident in these examples and throughout my own experience
in CILA, students were continually given opportunities for the kind
of in-depth self-reflection that both changed and empowered us.
Project reports and presentations, case studies in related coursework,
student-led reflections in sharing sessions and retreats—all invited us
to claim our own voice and place ourselves freely and intentionally
within the mission that is the church. Again, such expressions
were often characterized by paradox and tension. Dane wrote of
the striking shift in language between the "newer" and "older"
members of CILA whom he interviewed about their motivations for
involvement in the group:

> [Newer members] use terms like "helping others,"
> "community service," "volunteer," and "community" . . .
> Older members (those who have been involved for 2–3
> years) use the same terms, but much more frequently

---

56 Joe Marino, "St. Lucia 1973" (September 1973), 19.
57 Marino, 24.

uses phrases like "social justice/injustice," "commitment," "concern," "spiritual formation," "growth," and "action."[58]

He noted that older members more frequently expressed feelings of powerlessness and frustration, experienced challenges to previous ways of thinking, and questioned the degree of their commitment to activities and to others. At the same time, though, he observed that older members had been able to cultivate attitudes of hopefulness and compassion, as "one becomes more realistic about what can be done and begins to acquire the tools necessary to deal with existing injustices."[59] My own service experience through CILA leads me to echo these words.

Third, cognizant of the life stage and needs of its participants, CILA provided a welcoming and safe space for flourishing amid the tensions and questions. I am deeply grateful to the advisors of CILA—faculty and administrators, clergy, religious and lay—for fostering this safe space to develop the reflective capacities of a transient population of undergraduate students. Don McNeill was an exemplary mentor and model for me; I also remember the wise guidance of Claude Pomerleau, C.S.C. Several mentor couples such as Jim and Mary Ann Roemer, Tom and Jeanne Swartz, Tjaard and Anne Hommes, and Ken and Penny Jamison welcomed me into their homes and showed me how they lived as families committed to faith and justice. Influenced by the renewals discussed earlier and striving themselves to live the Christian vocation, they were true partners with us as we struggled through the tensions and complexities. They equipped us for new and daunting experiences in our service projects; joined us in study, dialogue, and prayer that productively challenged our previous perceptions of the world; and, most of all, helped us to embrace the risk of mutuality among ourselves and with them in

---

58 Dane, 5.
59 Dane, 6.

shaping our community. With their guidance, we in CILA could become not only more deeply committed laity but also leaders able to sponsor such growth in others. The effects of such mentoring have been long-lasting for graduates of CILA and later expressions of social concern at Notre Dame.

The Church of Vatican II invited participation in the common journey of the "People of God," not as onerous duty but as joyful and loving response to the communion offered by God as Father, Son, and Holy Spirit.

> "God is love, and he who abides in love, abides in God and God in Him." But, God pours out his love into our hearts through the Holy Spirit, Who has been given to us; thus the first and most necessary gift is love, by which we love God above all things and our neighbor because of God.[60]

CILA embodied the invitation of Jesus to the disciples to "come and see." For young people encountering the many new stimuli of collegiate life, the attractiveness of CILA was reinforced by the hospitality of its community spirit, coupled with the message that the Christian lifestyle was one of joy as well as responsibility. Its ambiance was thus light-hearted as well as serious. I fondly recall the singing, dancing, laughter, and celebratory spirit that characterized CILA gatherings. After several decades, the lyrics of a favorite CILA song called "Reach Out" still sound in my ears, accompanied by several vigorously strumming guitars:

> Reach out, reach out
> My brothers and sisters, reach out.

---

60 *Lumen Gentium*, 42.

In giving and sharing, believing and caring,
Reach out, together reach out.

CILA's spirit of welcome evoked the "catholic" spirit of Vatican II, open and encompassing all humanity. Starting with ourselves as intentionally cultivated and mutually supportive community, we could find the Spirit-led energy to identify with the "joys and hopes, griefs and anxieties" of the world and respond to them.

Having spent a career engaged in pastoral ministry and forming others for such ministry, I know that CILA has had a lasting impact on my practice. I was lovingly apprenticed into active membership in the Body of Christ, joining my gifts with others' for the good of church and society. The 1978–1979 *CILA Handbook* stated that we members could "offer with enthusiasm an organization which has and will continue to change and enrich lives."[61] As I revisit that handbook today, I give thanks to God for working, through CILA, to change and enrich my life.

---

61 *CILA Handbook*, 1.

CHAPTER 3

Taking It to the Streets:
The Prophetic Vision of Msgr. Jack Egan
and Peggy Roach

Barbara Frey

*I*n November 1974, a steady flow of Notre Dame undergraduates found their way to Peggy Roach's office for the Catholic Committee on Urban Ministry on the eleventh floor of the Hesburgh Library. Initially, one young woman arrived to inquire about a diaconate center in Chicago. Shortly thereafter, two others showed up to request social justice contacts for upcoming Urban Plunge experiences in Omaha, Columbus, Milwaukee, Des Moines, and New York. Roach treated the students graciously, trying her best to understand their needs and interests and to arrange contacts with the busy social activists and clergy throughout the United States who were members of the Catholic Committee on Urban Ministry (CCUM), which she coordinated with Msgr. John Egan. After a few days, however, the mildly exasperated CCUM coordinator penned a note to their teachers, Fr. Don McNeill, C.S.C., and Fr. Claude Pomerleau, C.S.C., asking, "my friends . . . can't we bring some order to the chaotic way in which things seem to be proceeding?"[62]

---

62 Peggy Roach, memorandum, November 25, 1974.

Roach's moment of frustration was fleeting but highlighted the challenges involved in the emerging field of experiential learning that was being pioneered by Don McNeill and others at Notre Dame in the early 1970s. Inspired by the church's ministers of social justice, Don sought to open that world to many students at Notre Dame who were eager to walk side by side in the work. Making those connections between students and the church's community ministers depended on the goodwill of Roach and Egan, who, through their organization of CCUM, had made the University of Notre Dame the national epicenter of Catholic social justice ministry. The students who eagerly sought out Roach's help represented the formation of a multigenerational network of post–Vatican II social justice activists, laying the groundwork for Notre Dame's robust experiential learning agenda, with a committed body of students, faculty, and Catholic urban ministers driven by their shared vision of a more just world.

The 1970s were a distinct decade of Catholic social consciousness. Emboldened by the discussions and outcomes of Vatican II as well as the events of the US civil rights movement, progressive American clergy began to address social and racial justice issues in their communities with unprecedented vigor, partnering with laypeople and with a new spirit of ecumenical collaboration. At the heart of this movement was a short, fiery Irish priest from Chicago named John J. ("Jack") Egan. A diocesan priest who grew up in the alleys of Chicago,[63] Egan was known as the face of Catholic social justice ministry in the city starting in the late 1950s. From 1958 to 1969 he directed the Chicago Archdiocesan Office of Urban Affairs, which became a model for other urban ministry offices across the country.

Egan believed that the role of priests was not to stay enclosed in their sanctuary but to get out, walk around, and study their territory, "cataloguing the rotting outside staircases on firetrap buildings and

---

63   Margery Frisbie, *An Alley in Chicago: The Life and Legacy of Monsignor John Egan* (Franklin, WI: Sheed & Ward, 2002), xxviii.

the smelly hallways in once well-kept apartment buildings."[64] At heart, Egan was a community organizer. He trained in the mid-1950s with legendary organizer Saul Alinsky and then worked for the next decades representing the Catholic Church as an advocate for racial justice on the South Side of Chicago. Egan lost his first major fight as a community organizer when, in 1958, he was one of the lone voices speaking against the University of Chicago urban renewal project in Hyde Park–Kenwood. The federally funded effort to clear blighted properties from the area surrounding the politically powerful university went ahead over Egan's protestations without any plans for relocating more than twenty thousand poor and mostly African American residents.[65] Egan learned mightily from this loss about the need to build coalitions to take on the status quo, but he also gained respect. According to Tom Gaudette, an Alinsky-trained organizer, "He was the only guy willing to stand up to the university and to city hall."[66]

Egan's next effort to address racial injustice in Chicago was more successful. In the 1960s, with the financial support and institutional backing of the archbishop of Chicago, Cardinal Albert Meyer, Egan convinced Saul Alinsky to organize the Woodlawn Organization to increase the capacity of African American community leaders to represent their own interests in city politics, on issues from voting rights to housing. When the University of Chicago took further steps on its urban expansion project, the Woodlawn Organization undertook several impressive actions, including bringing ten busloads of folks to meet with Mayor Richard Daley at city hall. By exerting their strength in numbers, the organization gained a significant voice in the urban planning, including a commitment of five hundred units of public housing.[67]

Conscious of the social and political barriers facing African Americans, Egan was an active supporter of the civil rights movement.

---

64   Ibid., 150.
65   Ibid., 97.
66   Ibid., 106.
67   Ibid., 158–59.

In 1965, Egan traveled to Selma, where he marched arm in arm with Rev. Martin Luther King Jr.'s lieutenants, Rev. Ralph Abernathy and Rev. C.T. Vivian, to confront the awaiting Alabama troops. The Chicago newspapers prominently featured Egan's photo the next day, thus solidifying his reputation as a brave voice for racial justice. When Dr. King chose Chicago as the site of his movement's northern campaign against racism in 1966, Egan provided important connections for him with the Catholic Church and the broader community. Egan urged then newly appointed Chicago archbishop, Cardinal John Patrick Cody, to support Dr. King and wrote a speech that was delivered in the archbishop's name at the July 1966 rally at Soldier Field.

Archbishop Cody, however, was not appreciative of Egan's visibility with regard to civil rights and social justice issues, and, upon taking his position with the archdiocese in 1966, he reassigned the assertive organizer to be the pastor of Presentation parish, in the heart of the black community in the Lawndale neighborhood on Chicago's West Side. What was intended as a demotion or internal exile instead afforded Egan a platform for building a more vibrant civil rights community in Lawndale. Volunteers flocked to work at Presentation, drawing energy from the spiritual and social electricity that Egan generated.

The most significant volunteer of the Presentation era was a civil rights activist named Peggy Roach. Returning to Chicago from her position with the National Council of Catholic Women in Washington, DC, Peggy was attracted to Presentation as the hub of Catholic activism on race and poverty issues.[68] Like Egan, Roach had been in Selma and through her host family there she was exposed to the dehumanizing experience of life for African Americans in segregated Alabama. Roach worked actively on the civil rights bill while in Washington; then, ready to take on an even more profound

---

68 Ibid., 190.

commitment to fighting racism, she moved to the more activist Chicago-based National Catholic Conference on Interracial Justice.

Roach had known Egan through mutual social justice activities in Chicago, so his base of action at Presentation parish was a natural place for her to reconnect. Observing how Egan was drowning in the demands of stacks of correspondence, she undertook the much-needed role of organizing his paperwork: he dictated notes, she transcribed them, he signed, she posted. Because of Roach's field experience, her understanding of the power and reach of the Catholic Church and its agencies, and her wholehearted embrace of Egan's mission and vision, her relationship with Egan quickly became and stayed symbiotic for the rest of their lives.

Because of this special relationship and their shared commitment to social justice, the two were known in their work as "coministers," partners, or, simply, Jack and Peggy. He referred to Roach as "my right arm and half my brain."[69] This was not an understatement, according to Mary Ann Roemer, in recalling the relationship. Once, at a brunch together, "Jack was pontificating about something," which was causing Mary Ann to be slightly annoyed. When he paused to sip his drink, Mary Ann interjected, "You know something, Jack? You'd be nothing without Peggy Roach." Upon hearing this, Jack threw back his head and laughed with delight.[70]

Even with Roach's help, the work in Chicago took on even more demands as the turbulent sixties came to a close. Cardinal Cody's authoritarian style took its toll on the clergy, scores of whom made the decision to leave the priesthood. Egan provided a safe space at Presentation for many of his friends to work out their personal decisions about the priesthood, and he felt a great personal loss as they chose to leave, one by one.[71]

---

69   Ibid., xiii.
70   Telephone interview, May 20, 2016.
71   Frisbie, 214.

An additional crucible was the devastating assassination of Dr. King in April 1968 and the subsequent firestorm that engulfed Lawndale, burning hundreds of homes and buildings in Presentation parish. Roving bands looted stores and smashed car windows; nine civilians were killed and dozens more injured. National Guard troops and tanks rolled down the streets of the neighborhood while anxious teachers and ministers tended the church and school.[72]

Shouldering these burdens was a diminished Egan, who had already had one heart attack, in 1962. These events were threatening to send his health spiraling downward. Fortuitously, in spring 1969, Egan bumped into Reverend Theodore Hesburgh, C.S.C., president of the University of Notre Dame, at a coffee shop in O'Hare airport. The account of the meeting is legendary. Fr. Hesburgh remembered, "He looked awful: wan, drawn and pale. 'Jack,' I said, 'you look like my father's colorful expression "hell hit with a shovel."' He admitted things were going pretty badly so I came up with a radical suggestion: 'Why don't you come down to Notre Dame for a sabbatical year?'"[73] Fortunately for all involved, one year grew into thirteen years, during which Egan and Roach helped to establish a legacy of engaged learning that has benefitted generations of students since.

Egan and Roach moved their cominstry to the campus of Notre Dame in fall 1970. The university proved to be a fertile ground for study, planning, and strategy on urban ministry, and Egan and Roach shared those benefits with the organization closest to their hearts, the Catholic Committee on Urban Ministry (CCUM). The committee brought together key personnel from diocesan urban ministry offices across the country; it was composed of a broad spectrum of priests, nuns, and laypeople who were driving the church's agenda nationally for human rights and social justice. When Egan created the group in 1967, CCUM was just an ad hoc group

---

72   Ibid., 199–201.
73   Reverend Theodore Hesburgh, foreword to Frisbie, supra, note 2 at xxiii–xxv, March 7, 1991.

of twenty-five priests and Roach. The availability of Notre Dame
as a convening space led to the group's expansion. Egan and Roach
invited a core CCUM group to campus in fall 1970 to determine the
direction of the organization. Six months later, an expanded group
held its first of many annual conferences—to explore "a theology of
social action." The larger group included lay ministers and women
(besides Roach) for the first time.[74] According to Tom Gaudette,
who attended the March 1971 CCUM conference, "the atmosphere
was fun. Roach was the creator of the whole thing. Egan was up
front . . . This is where you met everybody: the unions, the gays, the
women who wanted to be cardinals . . . the poets, the workers, the
prisoners. This was real Church, working Church."[75]

At about the same time Egan and Roach were putting down their
social justice roots, another Chicago Irishman, Fr. Don McNeill, was
returning to Notre Dame with his newly minted doctorate in pastoral
theology from Princeton Theological Seminary. Don instantly found
his place among the social justice networks on campus. The son of the
nationally known radio personality by the same name, Don entered
the Holy Cross novitiate after a stint in the US Army in the late 1950s.
In contrast to Egan's short stature, Don stood six foot six inches, a
height that supported a brief basketball career for "Splinters" McNeill
(a bench-sitting reference) as a Notre Dame undergraduate. If his
height was imposing, Don's congenial personality was his defining
characteristic. He was quick with a smile and a wave, often generated
as he pedaled across campus on his bicycle from meeting to meeting, a
full head of wavy hair blowing in the breeze. Don eschewed the Roman
collar, wearing instead a sports jacket and shirt with no tie and donning
a simple Holy Cross pendant. His casual dress and easy manner made
him accessible to students, especially many female students, who felt

74 John J. Egan, Peggy Roach, and Philip J. Murnion, "Catholic Committee on Urban Ministry:
Ministry to the Ministers," *Review of Religious Research* 20, no. 3 (1979): 279–90.
75 Frisbie, supra, note 2 at 239–40.

uniquely valued and respected by this nonconforming priest so eager to include them in all aspects of pastoral ministry.

Don's own spiritual formation with figures including renowned moral philosopher Victor Frankel, pastoral theologian Fr. Henri Nouwen, and C.S.C. mentor Ted Hesburgh left him with a deep interest in faith-based experiential and interdisciplinary learning. Based on this formation, Don was inspired to craft theology courses at the intersection of faith and action, with titles such as Religion and Values, Theology and Community Service, and the Church and Social Action.

Don was intent on preparing students for the work of pastoral theology. According to Jay Brandenberger, "Don's pastoral circle was his students."[76]

Don had known Egan and Roach before they brought their joint enterprise to Notre Dame. He and his classmate Claude Pomerleau heard about Egan's and Roach's work at Presentation parish on the West Side of Chicago in the sixties and traveled to Chicago to experience it for themselves. The two young priests were enthralled with the community of social activists they witnessed at Presentation. Don remembered, "Jack was so engaged with people of color, fighting the good fight."[77] The experience was further punctuated in Don's memory because he and Claude got stuck in a snowstorm on their way back to Notre Dame, which forced them to pull the car over and take refuge at the home of a relative for the night.

Several years later after the pilgrimage to Presentation, Don reconnected with Roach and Egan and their urban ministry network, this time on the Notre Dame campus. With Egan's and Roach's guidance and assistance, Don's vision of educating students in Vatican II theology through experiential learning was about to become a reality. Don found a ready group of students to implement this vision in the Council on the International Lay Apostolate (CILA).

---

76   Telephone interview, May 25, 2016.
77   Telephone interview, May 19, 2016.

Founded by Fr. Larry Murphy, MM, and a handful of Notre Dame and St. Mary's students in 1961, CILA was a lay movement dedicated to Christian lay service.[78] The initial focus of the apostolate was international service work, including summer projects for students in Mexico and Peru. Ernie Bartell, C.S.C., CILA's first advisor, accompanied a group of Notre Dame students in 1962 to Aguascalientes, Mexico, ostensibly to help with construction of a church. According to Bartell, the project "was not well conceived or executed, although it boasted some distinguished alumni," including Fr. Monk Malloy, C.S.C., a future president of the university.[79] Bartell noted, "In the summer of '62 this type of project attracted quite a bit of attention, since the idea for the Peace Corps which Fr. Hesburgh had helped develop with members of the Kennedy administration was still very new and exciting."[80] Fr. Hesburgh was a strong supporter of CILA's initiatives, celebrating Mass with CILA members and holding discussions with them, on topics such as Catholic values, service, and international justice.[81]

The CILA summer service projects expanded to many US sites as well, including in Harlem, Harrisburg, Washington, DC, and South Bend. On campus, CILA formed a tight-knit community through its Sunday Masses, as well as regular retreats and social events. As one of the few co-ed activities on campus, CILA involved many St. Mary's women, although they were not allowed to serve as officers or to accompany the men on the service projects until 1966. Bartell recalled, "A number of parents of St. Mary's girls were a bit uneasy about allowing their daughters to travel with the Notre Dame students."[82]

The spirit of service in pursuit of social justice that permeated the CILA community beckoned to Don, who quickly became the

---

78 Mary Hawley, History of the Center for Social Concerns, unpublished manuscript, 1987, at 1.
79 Ernie Bartell, C.S.C., "Dialogue: Forum," *Council for the International Lay Apostolate Newsletter,* vol. 1, no. 3 (November 1974): 4–6.
80 Ibid.
81 CILA, letter to membership, October 19, 1973.
82 Bartell, supra, note 18 at 5.

organization's faculty advisor, working to open up new opportunities along with a talented and committed group of student officers, including Mike Maguire, Joe Marino, Mary Beckman, and Doug Allen. The mission of CILA in the early 1970s was "service through education within community."[83] McNeill was intentional about building up the educational component of that mission. He designed a course called Religion and Human Development, taught in fall 1973 with Hubert Horan, to complement the CILA summer service experience. The course requirements for students included keeping a log of their summer service activities and following that up in the fall portion of the class with a "Journal of Inquiry"—a signature component of any McNeill course—in which they could personally reflect upon their field experiences, the course readings, discussions in faculty homes, and other interviews. The writings of Fr. John Dunne, C.S.C., and Henri Nouwen provided the intellectual food for discussion.

Egan and Roach brought their time, energy, and inspiration to the growing student interest in social justice and experiential learning. Don noted that Egan and Roach were a "constant help, such a gift, and they kept my feet on the ground." They were regular speakers and participants at CILA retreats. Don remembers how Egan "talked to the students about their whole educational wellbeing" and how Roach made sure the students were really prepared to go into situations in the community.[84]

Perhaps Egan's and Roach's most far-reaching contribution to the social justice education of Notre Dame students was their willingness to make connections for them with their CCUM colleagues across the country. With every annual gathering at Notre Dame, CCUM grew larger; by 1975, seven hundred attended the annual conference,

---

83 *Council for the International Lay Apostolate Newsletter,* vol. 1, no. 3 (November 1974), at 2.
84 Don McNeill, C.S.C., telephone interview, May 19, 2016.

and the organization had three thousand members.[85] If Notre Dame offered CCUM a space to meet and grow, CCUM returned the favor by serving as a connection to the real world for the students. Interviews with CCUM members began to show up as requirements in Don's courses. Visiting CCUM guests were tapped to speak at events and classes. In his role as education officer for CILA, Jay Brandenberger and fellow CILA member Don Murphy organized events with status quo–busting CCUM leaders such as Harry Fagan, director of the Commission on Catholic Community Action from Cleveland, and Marjorie Tuite, O.P., one of the key organizers of the first International Women's Ordination Conference.

The direct link between students and CCUM members began to grow significantly in relation to the Urban Plunge program, a forty-eight-hour winter break immersion for students into the problems and possibilities of America's inner cities. Mary Ann Roemer recalled, "They were the ones who made the Urban Plunge fly—these were Jack's people, on the front lines of the church. They took on the Vatican II charge of partnership." The Urban Plunge started informally over Christmas break 1974, after Roach supplied her list of CCUM contacts to those students engaging her in the eleventh-floor library office. That first year, Egan took a few students to Chicago, and Harry Fagan hosted Kathy Osberger and Mary Beckman in Cleveland.[86] The experience caught on and grew exponentially, requiring coordination to ensure that the CCUM folks, as hosts, and the students, as guests, were each adequately prepared for the Urban Plunge. Don McNeill took steps to beef up the educational component of the experience, registering "Plungers" in his one-credit course, the Church and Social Action, with the usual McNeillian mix of reading, journaling, and discussion. The theology department provided more in-depth follow up courses as well, such as the Unseen

---

85 Frisbie, 242.
86 Mary Beckman, Notre Dame, IN, interview, May 27, 2016.

City, which Don cotaught with John Roos, from the political science department, and Thomas Swartz, from the economics department.

CCUM's success was integral to the Urban Plunge. As CCUM grew in numbers and reach, so did the possibilities for placing students. McNeill and Egan were systematic about bringing students together with CCUM partners. CILA students (including myself) were enlisted to make presentations at the fall CCUM conferences to plead for more Urban Plunge partners. By 1976, plunge organizers were offering to send one hundred participants to virtually any city in the nation, thanks to their CCUM contacts. In an *Observer* article intended to drum up student support, CILA officer Doug Allen sold the plunge to the student audience in this way: "They will meet people who can help broaden their understanding of the varieties of social action approaches in the area and be able to 'walk the streets' and become more familiar with some of the apparent and hidden results of injustice and poverty.'"[87]

Throughout the remainder of the 1970s, Notre Dame's programs in experiential learning continued to grow. The "Year Off Program," in which students left school to live and work in Latin America, led to the Latin American Program for Experiential Learning (LAPEL), which offered academic credit to students pursuing independent studies while working in Lima, Peru, or Santiago, Chile. Building upon the Urban Plunge model, CILA offered an increasing number of longer-term summer service projects in coordination with CCUM contacts. The Oakland Training Institute, supervised by one of Jack and Peggy's CCUM contacts, John Baumann, S.J., was a sought-after site for summer internships and hosted a string of CILA members, including Don Murphy, Mary Meg McCarthy, Stacy Hennessey, and myself.

In 1977, Don McNeill took the natural next step, integrating

---

87   Maureen Griffin, "CILA plans 'Urban Plunge' project," *Notre Dame Observer* (October 26, 1976) at 6.

the service, social justice, and academic programs under one roof, called the Center for Experiential Learning, connected to the Egan-Roach office: the Center for Pastoral and Social Ministry. The Center for Experiential Learning got its own office space on the eleventh floor of the library, next door to Egan and Roach. "It was just an exciting place," according to Mary Ann Roemer, who by then was coordinating summer service sites for Don. She remembers frequent visitors from CCUM, who brought their news from the streets to eleventh-floor offices. The Center for Experiential Learning existed for five years, until the 1982 establishment of the Center for Social Concerns. Mary Hawley noted especially the center's "circular learning" model, characterized by immersion experience followed by reflection leading to new insights and, ultimately, into further experiences.[88]

Beyond the practical connections, the Egan-Roach duo both inspired and tempered Notre Dame's young experiential learning movement. Mary Beckman observed that McNeill, Roach, and Egan shared a common vision about an engaged and expanded church that was active not only in serving the poor but also in working for more just and equitable societies. Andrea Smith Shappell added that each of the three leaders contributed a powerful set of skills to the experiential collaboration: Jack brought his "street cred" and contacts, Roach brought her organizational sense, and Don brought his circle of committed students and faculty.[89]

And, standing in support of the whole enterprise was Fr. Ted Hesburgh, a friend and protector of this formidable pastoral ministry team and the students who benefitted from it. The respect between Egan and Hesburgh was palpable. Egan accepted Hesburgh's initial invitation to Notre Dame and kept accepting further invitations to

---

88 Hawley, supra, note 17, at 6.
89 Telephone interview, May 23, 2016.

serve the university until 1983, when he and Roach returned to the Chicago archdiocese to run its office on ecumenism. "Blessed years," wrote Hesburgh, "great work on the part of Jack and his indomitable assistant, Peggy Roach."[90] Don also had a special relationship with Hesburgh, who had advised him personally and professionally at key moments. In 1967, when Don was trying to establish a role for himself after his ordination, Hesburgh "looked me in the eye and said you are doing great things but you need to get more education." Don followed his advice then, and on multiple occasions thereafter, and was gratified to have Hesburgh's support for his many projects over the years.

The institutional accomplishments of these guiding lights of Notre Dame's social justice community are a legacy that has borne seasons of fruitful engagement long since they have left their leadership posts. But what continues to be present for those of us who witnessed this emerging experiential learning community is the humanity of these prophetic individuals—heroes who transformed our lives and who were transformed in return.

The depths of their personal engagement can be seen touchingly in their personal relationships with the CILA students. Jay Brandenberger, for instance, recalled how McNeill and Egan were directly involved in constructing the postgraduation lay ministry experience for him and his friends Tom Basile, Joe Forman, and Ricky Flores. Don put the four in touch with Egan, who made the contacts and arrangements for them to run a school for undocumented students in Houston, Texas. In November 1978, Egan met the four young men for dinner during a visit to Houston. The group was excited to describe their accomplishments thus far with the daunting project he had assigned to them. The serious young activists were taken aback when Egan brushed these tales aside and challenged them to dig deeper: "Yes, yes, this work is great, but tell me: what

---

90 Hesburgh, supra, note 12.

do you want to be doing in ten years?" After their initial year with the school, Tom Basile and Joe Forman found themselves in difficult professional and financial circumstances and uncertain what their next moves should be. Egan's response was to pay several months of their Houston rent out of his own pocket, before reiterating his vocational advice to his struggling disciples: "I think that the Lord is going to help you a good bit more if you really make some serious plans for yourself or with some of the other fellas as to where you want to spend the next ten years."[91] Unsurprisingly, Basile, Forman, Flores, and Brandenberger all ended up in service and social justice professions in the fields of law and education.

Both Egan and McNeill were supportive of the spiritual and professional development of female students, many of whom were drawn to the service-toward-justice model. From his earliest days in the experiential movement on campus, Don surrounded himself with strong, talented women: Mary Ann Roemer, Kathleen Maas Weigert, Andrea Smith Shappell, Mary Meg McCarthy, and Stacey Hennessey, to name but a few. In Mary Ann's words, "Don was smart enough to listen to women, and he listened to me." Mary Beckman characterized Don's model as "inviting and inviting and inviting." Indeed, in Don's vision of the church, women were invited to speak, to organize, and to preach.

Egan was a generation older than Don, and his views about women took longer to evolve. Despite the central role of Roach in his life and his life's work, Egan did not challenge the diminished role of women in the institutional church that he loved. Egan extolled the role of religious sisters and the laity in the work of the church but did not push for more. In a keynote presentation to the Daughters of Charity Conference on "Action in Ministry" in April 1978, Egan exclaimed, "Sisters, we know that one of the most exciting results of

---

91   Letter from Msgr. John Egan to Tom Basile, Notre Dame, IN, April 21, 1980.

Vatican II . . . is the understanding that all baptized Christians are called to minister in the Church."[92] He observed that "as Daughters of Charity you are pastoral ministers of a special kind" and noted that "the world more than ever needs the liberated woman and the Church needs her, too," but did not go any further to assess the institutional limitations on their role in the church.[93]

During Egan's years at Notre Dame, he came into contact with a number of female students who looked to him as a mentor. Egan was generous with his time in personal meetings and correspondence with these young women and advocated on their behalf. After graduation, former CILA Chair Mary Beckman, for example, worked with Catholic Charities in New York, with one of Jack and Peggy's CCUM contacts. Mary wrote Jack in August 1976 about her call to work more deeply "for Church change, change so that Church can more fully bring about a more just world." She told him about her excitement at the Women's Ordination Conference and how she sensed "the presence of the Spirit amidst that group of women!"[94] Egan's response was not enthusiastic. He wrote, "While I understand the emotion of the moment, I always looked upon you as not only a person of great reason but also a person who would have such a great love for the institutional Church that for you to say that I feel I could have gone on to say Mass causes me a bit of pause." Despite Egan's concerns, he went out of his way to put Mary in touch with his contacts all over the world in relation to her proposed undertaking to study the activities of the global church in response to Vatican II, including the role of women in the Catholic Church.[95]

A lifetime of working side by side with talented women, including

---

92   Msgr. John Egan, "Address to the Daughters of Charity Conference," St. Louis, MO, April 20, 1978, at 10.
93   Ibid., 11, 14.
94   Mary Beckman, letter to Msgr. John Egan, August 23, 1976.
95   Msgr. John Egan, letter to various contacts, December 6, 1977.

students, sisters, and his cominister, Roach, ultimately changed Egan's views on the role of women in the church. Twenty-five years after he wrote with concern about the desire of his young mentee to "say Mass," Egan penned his "Last Testament," published posthumously in the *National Catholic Reporter* in 2001. In the piece, Egan underscored the sixty-six years of priesthood he had devoted to "thorny problems of social justice," before concluding, "Now, I have to ask our church to open its eyes and lift its voice on behalf of another justice issue—the church's commitment to the broadest possible inclusion of women in positions of leadership and authority in the church, including further study and discussion of the ordination of women."[96]

Egan and Roach were instrumental to the founding of the Center for Social Concerns at the University of Notre Dame in 1983 by Don and CILA students as an outgrowth of all the service learning and social action programs on campus. Roach served throughout the 1980s on the advisory board of the center and provided a voice of experience about potential community-based projects for students. Don remembers that, in his role as the new center's director, Roach kept him in line, responding to some of his ideas with, "No, Don, that wouldn't work." Roach remained a steadfast partner to Jack in all of his activities back in Chicago, in the archdiocese, and with DePaul University. Despite her unassuming nature, Roach was publicly recognized for her own enormous contributions to the social justice agenda that Egan spearheaded. When the bishop presiding at Egan's 2001 funeral acknowledged Roach, the more than two thousand in attendance rose to their feet and gave her an extended ovation. "We were quite a team," said Roach.[97] Quite a team.

---

96 Msgr. John Egan, "Use the Gifts God Gives: the Last Testament of Monsignor John J. Egan," *National Catholic Reporter* (June 1, 2001), accessed July 14, 2016, http://www.womenpriests.org/teaching/egan.asp.

97 Robert Ludwig, "Preface to this Memorial Edition," in Frisbie, ix–xviii, at xiii.

CHAPTER 4

Walk the Walk

Stacy Hennessy

Within weeks of arriving at Notre Dame as a transfer student in the fall of 1979, I came across 1.5 LaFortune Center. This is an impossible office to "trip over." One would find it only if he or she were intentionally seeking the destination; that's how far out of the way it was. The office was oddly titled "Volunteer Services," and I was looking for a way to get involved. I'm not sure what I expected, but after all, this is Notre Dame, the great Catholic university committed to faith and, I assumed, justice. Whatever I had imagined, this space, while intimate and cozy, stretched the definition of "office." It was small—really small. There was a waiting area that extended the length of the room, perhaps fifteen feet wide. On the left wall, there was a low-lying bookshelf with the latest copies of magazines I had never heard of: *Sojourners*, *Bread for the World*, and *Oxfam*. To my immediate right was a closed door that might have been mistaken for a coat closet except there was signage and a bulletin board: "Mary Ann Roemer, Holy Cross Associates." On the bulletin board there was a global map with pushpins in the locations where volunteer groups were currently serving, hosted by Holy Cross. I picked up a brochure.

At the other end of the room there was another office, which looked substantially larger, and on the door was a metal plate: "Sr. Judith Anne Beattie, Director." While I was taking all of this in and deciding whether to stick around and wait for a human being to show up, the door to my right sprung open and a student engulfed in laughter emerged, eclipsing Mrs. Roemer, who, small in stature but not in character, was easily masked by the broad-shouldered, joyful boy. The student darted off, and she caught my eye. "Hi!" she exclaimed. "I'm Mary Ann." I might have said hi, but I probably said, "How do you get to go there?" and pointed to Nairobi. "Oh! Well, are you a senior?" I wasn't. "Well, you have to be a graduating senior." She explained the program in brief and asked whether I wanted to come in her office, which I did not, and would I like more information. I said sure, and she encouraged me to continue a relationship with her if I was seriously interested.

So it began. A conversation, a bulletin board, and a lifetime of change.

Through Mary Ann I became connected to Fr. Don McNeill and the staff at the Center for Experiential Learning: Marcia LeMay, Andrea Shappell, Reg Weissert, Mary Meg McCarthy, and Kathy Osberger. Eventually, my work-study assignment on the slop line in South Dining Hall was redirected to Fr. Don's office, which gave me more time to join CILA, the Community for International Lay Apostolate, the Farm Workers movement with Cece Schickel, and World Hunger Coalition, ably directed by Will O'Brien. I began attending meetings, retreats, service projects, and the Urban Plunge. I spent a summer as a community organizer in Oakland, California. At times, Mary Meg and I would have dinner at the Roemers', always preceded by Mass with Fr. Don and a meal in which everyone had a hand. At the table Jim Roemer would open up a vast conversation with a single question, for example: "If you could address any world issue in which you believe real change is possible, what would it be?"

And the discussion would go on for hours, until someone suddenly realized that we had a hundred and fifty pages of reading to do, or a paper to write, or a friend we had promised to meet. The friendships deepened, but so too did my commitment to justice and desire for community: breaking bread, sharing hope, and effecting change— one meal at a time.

I split the bulk of my time between 1.5 LaFortune Center and the ninth floor of the library—that is, until the spring of 1980. Fr. Don asked Mary Meg and I whether we would meet with him about an idea he had. So we did. Ever the starving, broke college students, we opened a jar of peanut butter and a pack of saltines and listened to Don's idea. "What if," he began, "we combined 1.5 LaFortune Center with the ninth floor of the library and made the two offices one office?" But the difference between Mary Ann and Judith's offices and Don's was great. Whereas Mary Ann had no furniture in her office save a tiny side table that she used as a desk and lots of floor cushions upon which to sit cross-legged and chat, Don's offices were sterile and serious—productive in a way that universities value. When I first reported to work, for example, Don was proofing the galleys for the book *Compassion,* which he wrote with Henri Nouwen. In short, 1.5 LaFortune was all heart and home and nurturing for students exploring service; ninth floor was coursework, bookwork, and head work on justice and peace. We explained to Don that both were important but not well integrated at the time.

When the point was made, Don responded, "Exactly. We need to integrate the head and the heart. We need to make the point that service is at the heart of who we are as a Catholic university. Otherwise, Notre Dame will only be known for sports and academics. But the mission of the Gospel is more than that." We tossed that around for a bit, and Mary Meg asked the critical questions, "How?" and "Where?" The "where" was much more easily answered.

Don knew that the WNDU TV/radio station was being moved from its location adjacent to the library to a new building off US 31. Several departments were bidding for the building. Don's idea was that Mary Meg and I would spearhead the proposal to convert the old WNDU space into a Center for Social Concerns. This is how well Don had thought this through before going public: the acronym for the center would be C.S.C., establishing a clear connection to the Congregation of Holy Cross.

The longer we talked, the more excited we got—except there was a problem. Mary Meg was a second-semester senior, and her time was pretty limited. But there Don corrected us. He had identified the two of us because we both had training in community organizing. So what Don was asking was, "Could you organize a student/faculty movement?" We looked at each other, only a little terrified, and then at Don and said, "Sure!" The walk back to campus was much farther than it had been a couple of hours before. But by the time we arrived at Walsh, we had a list of students to be contacted and a list of faculty members that we thought would be instrumental. Don's job was to get a meeting with Msgr. Egan about fine-tuning a campus-wide plan, and we set to work.

The spring of 1979 was spent plotting and planning, "canvassing" the campus, and meeting with students one-on-one until we had a significant buy-in from ten, twenty, fifty, a hundred students. We had identified "sure supporters," individuals in their senior (or, preferably, their junior) years, who were already spearheading student movements for peace and justice. We used the mailing list from the past few Urban Plunge enrollments as a list of possible supporters, and we worked with the center staff to come up with scripts and talking points that were accurate and persuasive.

The turning point came again with Mary Meg. She thought that the best way to convince students that this was not just a good idea but a GREAT idea—an ESSENTIAL idea—was to draw up plans for the former WNDU building as we imagined it would be, as a center for volunteerism and experiential learning. Enter a fifth-year architecture student named Paul Kapczuk, who clearly loved Mary Meg. He agreed to draw up what became five renderings of the converted space. We met initially to discuss what should go into the building—a welcoming lobby, a kitchen/coffee house, workspace for student leaders of service groups and outreach, offices for staff and faculty, a large meeting room/classroom, a chapel, and a library or reading room. Then he went to town designing the space. We found that once the drawings were done, students were much more supportive, if not enthusiastic, about the prospects, and then we were ready for the big faculty showdown.

Don had arranged for one hundred plus faculty members to meet, and he had on the agenda himself, me, Mary Meg, Sister Judith Anne, and Fr. Jack Egan. The meeting was pretty tense because campus space at Notre Dame, especially premium space next to the library, was coveted. Resources were limited and hopes were high within every department for expansion and visibility. But after a one-hour meeting, when Fr. Jack got up and talked about the civil rights movement and talked about the need for Catholic universities across the country to take a stand—to stand in and with the Gospel, not for materials and pride—there was a shift in tone until he had everyone standing arm-in-arm singing "We Shall Overcome."

The final stage was a private meeting with Fr. Ted Hesburgh. Fr. Ted would see only three students at a time, so Paul, Mary Meg, and I were selected. We scripted our remarks and rehearsed the presentation over and over again. When the time came, we put on our "Sunday best" and headed up to the top floor. When we arrived, we were informed by Helen that Fr. Hesburgh was detained but that he would see us shortly. She informed Father that we had arrived, and to our great surprise he said, "Oh, tell them to come in! I want them to meet Bobby!" So the door to his office flew open, and the introductions began. "Meet Robert Kennedy Jr." There we were, in the private office of the great Theodore Hesburgh with the son of the great Senator Robert Kennedy. If I had had words before, they were gone now.

Suddenly, we were alone with Fr. Ted, who enthusiastically asked what he could do for us and plopped down in his chair, directing his full attention in our direction. "Father," Mary Meg began, "we have come to make a proposal to you about the use of the WNDU building that is being vacated next year."

He immediately retorted, "Well, a lot of people want that building—A LOT of people. What makes you think your idea is better than theirs?" I'm not sure what Mary Meg said, but I think she said something including the words "Catholic," "justice," and "service," at which Fr. Hesburgh raised his eyebrows. I am not so naive as to think that this was the first mention of our idea to Fr. Ted. Fr. Jack and Fr. Don would have had ample time to mention the idea in passing over dinner at Corby Hall. Nonetheless, encounters with undergraduates were near and dear to his heart, and if we could be both articulate and persuasive with Fr. Ted, we might gain an edge over our competition. And so we began. We had four minutes until his next appointment.

Mary Meg laid out the idea for the building and why its location was essential to the work of service—visibility was essential. Students who might never consider service as part of their Notre Dame experience couldn't help but see the center on their way to the library and out of curiosity stop by for a lecture, or a cup of coffee, or just because. Paul then started in with the drawings. The integration of classroom learning, service, a chapel, and a kitchen clearly sparked an interest for Fr. Ted. And I concluded with the real mission of a Catholic university, which is to imitate Christ, and what better way to do that than through service and justice.

As soon as I concluded, he jumped up and said, "Great! Great! This is terrific! I'll take this up with the board." And off we went. We flew down the steps of the Main Building, and Paul ran to class while Mary

Meg and I tried to reach Don from Walsh Hall. No word. There was very little time left in the semester now, and Mary Meg and Paul really had to turn their attention to finals and plans for the future. But so much had happened in so short a period of time that it was pretty hard to imagine any of this ending badly.

When I returned to campus in the fall after a summer of service, Fr. Don, Sr. Judith Anne, and myself had been invited by the board of trustees to make a proposal to them about the use of the WNDU building. No student had ever been invited to address the board. We credited Hesburgh with the bold invitation and set out to prepare our scripted remarks. Judith was very apprehensive. As the idea for the center gained momentum, she began to feel that in creating a larger institution of service and learning, spirituality would get lost, that students would get all busy in the "doing" and forget to reflect on why we do what we do or how this serves the greater vision of the Kingdom. She wasn't getting cold feet so much as expressing a deep concern about the reality of culture and campus life. At the time all I could feel was a loss of support, but in retrospect, I am now able to see and understand her prophetic voice. Today I would say that, yes, something was definitely lost in the creation of the Center for Social Concerns, but so, so much more was gained.

As was the one-on-one meeting with Fr. Ted, the meeting with the board was brief and to the point. Don spoke about location, Holy Cross identity, alumni support, and student/faculty interactions. Judith reported on the numbers of students involved in service, volunteer opportunities, summer projects, and postgraduate projects and the room for growth given that there was far more demand than two staffers could meet. And I spoke, again, to the mission of a Catholic university and what service-learning had done for me and my relationship to God, to the church, and to the poor, and that I was forever indebted to Notre Dame for giving me the eyes to see what Christ asks all of us to see.

Aside from speaking engagements with Don and Judith before alumni clubs in the Chicago area to see whether there would be any money available to fund such a project, my senior year was focused primarily on advancing the causes of justice and service on campus. No decision was made on the WNDU building during the academic year 1980–1981. I left for Chile on a Holy Cross Associates project in late July of 1981. In the fall of that year it was announced that the building would become the Center for Social Concerns. The renovations of the building bore a striking similarity to Paul's renderings. And in the spring of 1983 when the building was dedicated, Mary Meg was the speaker.

Today that building has been torn down. Now in its place stands a beautiful structure that houses much more than just the Center for Social Concerns. I'm sure that's a good thing for the university. I feel conflicted about what it is for students. The Center for Social Concerns was a project of the times. There were no cell phones or flat screens or portable devices of any kind. The center was built on personalism: personally reaching out person to person with a line that began something like, "Hey, have you heard about . . . ?" Such things are no longer common, but regularly Mary Ann Roemer would place a sandwich board in the middle of the sidewalk in front of the center with colorful signage and even more colorful helium balloons attached, inviting passersby to a coffee house, or a film screening, or a political debate, and students and faculty would come. Regularly, students would arrange to meet in front of the center and take advantage of free coffee and the off chance that there was free food in the always-open kitchen. In distress over the sudden outbreak of war, students would wander up the stairs and take time alone in the chapel. There hung a stained glass piece called "Bread and Roses." The staff met there once a week to pray together, to reground our work in the Gospel, and to not get too carried away with the issues of the day. It was flooded with sunlight, informal, and even loud at times. I miss that.

As projected, the Center for Social Concerns has taken its place at the heart of the University of Notre Dame. With great regularity the president of the university touts statistics on the number of undergraduates involved in service and the number who go on to do service after graduation. Included in these numbers might be those who choose to go into public service as a result of an experience they had during an Urban Plunge in freshman year, or a life-changing encounter at the Center for the Homeless, or a truly humbling experience at Logan Center, in Nairobi, or San Salvador. It is not enough, as it turns out, to talk the talk. On a cold night in January over a jar of peanut butter and saltine crackers, Don McNeill was right. We have to walk the walk.

CHAPTER 5

Contemplation and Action: Conversations with Sr. Judith Anne Beattie, C.S.C., and Mary Ann Roemer

Margaret Pfeil

"There is no contradiction between action and contemplation when Christian apostolic activity is raised to the level of pure charity. On that level, action and contemplation are fused into one entity by the love of God and of our brother [and sister] in Christ . . . The most important need in the Christian world today is this inner truth nourished by this Spirit of contemplation: the praise and love of God, the longing for the coming of Christ, the thirst for the manifestation of God's glory, his truth, his justice, his Kingdom in the world." —Thomas Merton[98]

*B*eginning in 1976, Sr. Judith Anne Beattie, C.S.C., and Mary Ann Roemer worked with Fr. Don McNeill to establish the Office of Volunteer Services, which would eventually be folded into the newly created Center for Social Concerns in 1983. A central focus of their ministry was to help students connect contemplation and action, theory and praxis, faith and justice by helping them to develop disciplined habits of reflection. Distilled from recent

---

98   Thomas Merton, *Contemplative Prayer* (Garden City, NY: Image Books, 1971), 115.

interviews with Judith Anne and Mary Ann, this essay explores their holistic approach to student formation.[99]

From 1976 to 1984, Judith Anne worked with student service groups, assisting them with practical things as well as matters of the heart. She remembers CILA as an exemplary model of formation: "It was the only student group that combined service, summer immersion work, regular theological reflection, justice education, and retreats." They focused in particular on the issues of armed conflict in Central America and nuclear disarmament. Henri Nouwen directed a few of their retreats, as well as Sr. Helena Brennan, who had worked as a missionary in Nigeria.

Service and theological reflection were also consistent elements of Don's community-based learning courses. Grounded in pastoral theology, he used case studies to help students develop a theory of praxis. As still happens today in the Summer Service Learning Program, students processed summer service projects either through short meetings with faculty and staff or by taking a three-credit theology course first taught by Don and now offered by other professors on the CSC staff.

This reflection process bore fruit in students' discernment of life choices, Judith Anne remembers. Some took paths of service to economically challenged areas of the world, and others pursued a particular career trajectory related to their majors, practicing it in a way that served the marginalized. "There are many ways to live out the insights you arrive at if you have been formed to do so."

Judith Anne emphasized the critical role that Mary Ann played in accompanying students, guiding them in the process of discernment around life choices, including postgraduate service options such as the Holy Cross Associates: "A developmental task of college-age students is to separate oneself from one's parents,

---

99   Judith Anne Beattie, interview, April 28, 2016; Mary Ann Roemer, interview, June 1, 2016.

to undertake one's own journey, not what parents desire for them but what they feel called to do." Some students faced a serious challenge in discussing their process with their parents, many of whom felt blindsided by seemingly sudden shifts in their children's postgraduate plans. As they struggled to understand, they too were being formed alongside their children, and Mary Ann, as a parent, could empathize with them and also be an important listening presence for the students.

Mary Ann deeply values the mutuality she experienced in this ministry: "The students helped me. I was a better person, a better mother, and I was able to learn more about the social action of the church." This mutuality extended to her relationship with Don McNeill as a priest and colleague: she and other staff were able to express their views honestly with him, and he valued that open, deliberative communication process. She perceived this kind of authentic collaboration as part of the fruit of Vatican II: laypeople were able to exercise greater agency in ministerial work in service of the church's mission, and the CSC staff were modeling that process for students as well as for the wider university community.

For students experiencing crises of faith, Mary Ann said, the CSC "offered a way to be in the church," symbolized well by the *aggiornamento* of Vatican II, an open door of invitation to a broader understanding of lay vocation. "The CSC became a safe place for the seekers, who were not sure whether there was room in the church for their questions, for their desire to take action to support the cause of justice." A seeker herself, Mary Ann cultivated a safe space for students to voice their doubts and musings.

"The joys and the hopes, the griefs and the anxieties of the men [and women] of this age, especially those who are poor or in any way afflicted, these too are the joys and hopes, the griefs and anxieties of the followers of Christ. Indeed, nothing genuinely human fails to raise an echo in their hearts."[100] These opening lines of *Gaudium et Spes* were a source of consolation and encouragement for the CSC's seekers. Drawn through compassionate love to identify with those suffering in the world and wondering about the role of the church in that process, students were seeking the sort of integration of God's love and justice that Merton suggested in the quotation above, perhaps without being able to articulate that desire.

As students wrestled with questions of faith, justice, and love—and, ultimately, questions of theodicy—Vatican II profoundly shaped the CSC's approach to formation, Judith Anne noted. "*Gaudium et Spes* emphasized facing the modern world, and all baptized Christians have a piece to contribute in the church," she said. "No matter what your work is, it is contributing to building the Kingdom of God . . . It is not [a question of] secular vs. sacred."

As Barbara Frey described in her chapter, Msgr. Jack Egan used this Vatican II vision to develop his urban ministry, and the CSC actively fostered student collaboration with his work as a way of pastorally relating to church issues in the wider world. Through CILA, students were exposed to community organizing with PICO in California. There they acquired skills necessary to address justice issues.

"Faith-based Christian formation is a significant contribution of the CSC," Judith Anne said. From the beginning, the CSC encouraged integration of Catholic social teaching, starting with theological reflection on *Populorum Progressio*, the bishops' texts on Appalachia, and the US bishops' 1983 pastoral letter, *The Challenge of Peace*: "Students didn't just read documents but also had the experience of encountering and accompanying people." Visitors from Central America were "living texts," she remembers, and the CSC became known as a welcoming space of hospitality that

---

100 *Gaudium et Spes,* para.1.

nurtured relationships. "To have a space like the coffeehouse was important for the CSC. People who normally would never intersect could come together."

Judith Anne, Mary Ann, and Don took seriously Merton's admonition: "[One] who attempts to act and do things for others or for the world without deepening [one's] own self-understanding, freedom, integrity and capacity to love will not have anything to give to others."[101] As Judith Anne puts it, "You can go everywhere and be nowhere unless you do something with what happens." For that reason, their ministry emphasized particular aspects of the formation process using Peter Henriot's model of the pastoral circle: service, analysis, theological reflection, justice education, and prayer were key components of the CSC's work from the beginning. "It is important to take one's experience seriously, asking questions of it and noticing what it is asking of you," Judith Anne said. "It starts from the experiential, rather than the usual starting point of academics in the world of ideas. Intellectual formation is important, but there has to be more to formation . . . Head, hearts, and hands—formation has to go that full circle." They understood that many students launched into service without deeper reflection, but their goal was to help them move along a spectrum toward more holistic integration.

Henri Nouwen's work was critically important in spiritual formation of students because he held contemplation and action together, Judith Anne said. "It was important to get students to stop going from one thing to another without reflection. In his book on silence, Thich Nhat Hanh addresses nonstop chatter. This includes not just talking with others but within one's own head." Going away on retreat, as the CILA participants did, interrupted the stream of constant motion and noise. "It was the sort of displacement that Henri and Don talked about in *Compassion*."

101 *Contemplation in a World of Action* (Notre Dame: University of Notre Dame Press, 1998), 160.

In addition to attending Henri's talks and retreats, the CSC staff encouraged students to adopt regular practices of reflection. Journaling was particularly valuable in cultivating contemplative awareness, and Don incorporated it into his courses. "Getting students into journaling, reading, and using the case study model helped them to reflect and connect their experience with theology, the Gospel, and spirituality," Judith Anne said. She hopes that the faith formation piece continues in the CSC's work "so that students pay attention to discernment around how to give one's life away for the sake of the Gospel."

In helping students to integrate action and contemplation, Judith Anne highlighted particular signs she looks for in a person's life journey as she accompanies him or her, such as seminal or peak experiences. "When you look back at your journey, were there one or two things you wanted to be or do? Was there someone who inspired you, and what drew you to them? Where do you find your passion and energy? What draws you in the Gospels, in spiritual reading? What do you read? How does your style of prayer lead you out to one's brothers and sisters, and how does your work with people lead you to prayer? These questions help to identify threads in a person's experiences." In sitting with a student after an immersion experience, she could sense whether something had touched him or her, and she encouraged the student to reflect on it. "The hope is that a person will develop habits of reflection through prayer, journaling, spiritual direction, and talking with friends or a mentor. Being part of a community of reflection is important."

The CSC staff tried to model what they were asking of students by consistently praying and reflecting together as a community. Eucharist was part of their rhythm, and the staff went on spiritual retreat together. Don also led faculty and staff trips to Mexico with regular follow-up meetings that included potluck meals, Mass, and conversation about justice education issues. "It was ongoing adult formation," Judith Anne remembers.

Merton wrote, "What matters is the contemplative orientation of the whole life of prayer . . . Prayer must penetrate and enliven every department of our life, including that which is most temporal and transient."[102] Elsewhere in this volume, contributors acknowledge awkward, humorous, and even somnolent experiences of communal prayer in Associate households. But, even in those moments, there was still a kind of formation under way, as Judith Anne and Mary Ann have suggested: their approach to holistic formation centered on helping students develop disciplined *habits* of reflection and integration and to understand it as a process rather than a destination or a goal. That kind of contemplative awareness, cultivated over time, results in the sort of deeper contemplative orientation of prayer life, and really all aspects of one's life, to which Merton alluded. Ultimately, Judith Anne, Mary Ann, Don, and their CSC colleagues were attempting to invite students and faculty into *a way of being in the world*, bringing contemplative awareness into every aspect of their lives as part of what it meant to be a Christian disciple in the modern world, sharing in its joys and hopes, griefs and anxieties, and finding God there, and within themselves, and in all those around them. It is all one whole, in which action and contemplation become united in and through the grace of God's love, as Merton described.

---

102 Merton, *Contemplative Prayer* (Garden City, NY: Image Books, 1971), 114–115.

CHAPTER 6

Holy Cross Associates and Formation in Lay Vocation

Matt Feeney

I graduated from Notre Dame in 1979 and from 1979 to 1980 served as a Holy Cross Associate in Phoenix, where I taught at St. Matthew Catholic School. I met my wife, Michele, at Notre Dame Law School, which I attended following my HCA year. In 1983, I joined Snell & Wilmer, a large Phoenix-based law firm, where I serve as the managing partner today. Michele and I married in 1984, and we have five children—Maureen, Colleen, Michael, Rus, and Joseph—and one grandchild, Margaret Rose Wynn, or "Maggie," who was born in April 2016.

From the vantage point of time, I see that many of my life's threads, at least those of which I am most proud, lead back to my year as a Holy Cross Associate. Three of these threads include selected life lessons, service to the poor, and my lifelong collaboration with the Congregation of Holy Cross.

I entered Notre Dame in 1975. While there, I met extraordinarily good people, many of them priests, including Fr. Eugene Gorski, C.S.C., the rector of my dormitory, Howard Hall. He was a tall, thin, white-haired man with a white beard and an upper-crust bearing.

He was an articulate and elegant professor who intently listened to his students' questions and comments. He kept the door to his modest living room open well past midnight every day so that Howard Hall residents could wander in to speak with him. He would listen to their problems and frequently exclaim, "It's the human condition!" That statement oftentimes pulled students from the abyss of loneliness to the community of broken humankind.

Fr. Gene was a believer in grace, redemption, and "working out your salvation with diligence."[103] He would oftentimes quote Voltaire's *Candide*, which he had read in the original French as a Holy Cross seminarian: "Cultivate your garden."

I cultivated my musical garden at Notre Dame. My roommate, Steve Podry, taught me how to play the guitar. Beginning our sophomore year, Steve, I, and other friends would provide music at the Howard Hall Saturday night midnight Mass, which was always a packed event followed by cookies and drinks. Those Masses built community, plumbed serious theological and social issues, and sparked my interest in pursuing my burgeoning spirituality.

Unlike many of my classmates who were naturally drawn to postgraduate volunteer programs, I was not involved in "service projects" while at Notre Dame. I quietly cultivated my spiritual garden by reading *The Way of a Pilgrim* (an influential book), attending Mass, discussing life's big issues with my friends, and writing occasional "Howard Hall Mass Songs" with my friend Carl Casazza. My Notre Dame life, which was rich and transformative in so many ways, marched on to my senior year (1978–1979), when I thought I would attend law school following graduation.

The Nazz was a student coffeehouse located in the basement of Notre Dame's LaFortune Student Center. In the 1970s the Nazz

---

103 In the introduction to Fr. Gene's 2007 book, *Theology of Religions: A Sourcebook for Interreligious Studies* (Paulist Press), Fr. Gene posed a typically thoughtful question: "Might it be that the one true God—The Father, Jesus in the Spirit—is active in [the other great religions of the world], working out the divine plan of salvation?"

Fr. Don McNeill with other seminarians at Collegio di Santa Croce in Rome, September 1963

Fr. Don McNeill and Fr. Claude Pomerleau with friends in Rome, shortly after their ordination

Fr. Don McNeill and Fr. Claude Pomerleau at the equator in Uganda

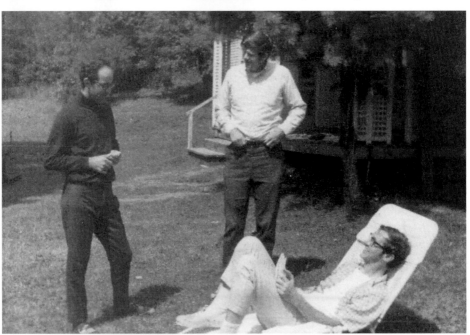

Fr. Henri Nouwen and Fr. Don McNeill on retreat with a friend

Front Row (from left): Jan Vining, Maura O'Malley, and Mary Beth Simons

Back Row (from left): Jim Ladner and Matt Feeney

Members of the Holy Cross Associates advisory board (Moreau Seminary, April 1983). Fr. Don McNeill, C.S.C., seated at the middle of the table, was the HCA program director at the time. Mary Ann Roemer sits to Fr. Don's right. Matt Feeney, who assisted Fr. Don in administering the HCA program while he attended Notre Dame Law School, is in the back row, second from the right.

Fr. Ted Hesburgh blessing the
first CSC building with Fr. Don
McNeill in the background

Fr. Ted Hesburgh
and Fr. Henri Nouwen

Fr. Henri Nouwen giving a talk on campus

Kathleen Maas Weigert visiting with guests in the CSC coffeehouse

Pax Christi Peace Vigil at the dedication of the Clarke Memorial Fountain on Notre Dame's campus, 1986

Fr. Don McNeill speaking with a group in the old CSC classroom

Fr. Don McNeill, executive director of the CSC, 1993

Rectors' lunch at the CSC coffeehouse

Fr. Henri Nouwen
with Fr. Don McNeill

CSC student activities gathering

Fr. Don McNeill facilitates a discussion following the Urban Plunge experience

Student discussion outside the old CSC building, 1997

CSC Staff Photo, 2003

Margaret Pfeil and Laura Beverly welcome Bob Snyder and other members of the CSC's advisory council to the Catholic Worker community in South Bend, 2011

Students engage in discussion as part of the Inside Out course offered at Westville Correctional Facility

Young companions on mission!

Students engaged in a CSC service project

Members of the early CSC team visit the newly opened Geddes Hall

From left to right: Marcia LeMay, Andrea Smith Shappell, Kathy Royer, Fr. Don McNeill, Mary Ann Roemer, Regina Weissert, and Sr. Judith Anne Beattie, C.S.C.

Fr. John Jenkins, university president, greets a student at the annual CSC Postgraduate Service Send-off

Bonnie Bazata, director of a local community agency, Bridges out of Poverty, gives a presentation in the CSC coffeehouse

Fr. Don McNeill, drumming with the Notre Dame Folk Choir at a CSC celebration

Deer Park gathering (Deer Park, Maryland, July 26, 1998). Fr. John Dunne, C.S.C., back left with the hat, gave a talk entitled "The Spiritual Journey"; Don McNeill is in the back right; Matt Feeney is in the second row from the back, to Fr. Dunne's left, holding one-year old Mike Feeney, who began his freshman year at Notre Dame in August 2016; Michele Feeney is directly in front of Fr. Dunne; and Mary Ann Roemer is directly in front of Michele

From left: Neal Mongold (a Notre Dame classmate and Howard Hall midnight Mass singer), Matt Feeney, Fr. Eugene Gorski, and Steve Podry (South Bend, June 1, 2014); Fr. Gene died January 3, 2015, following a brief illness

Front Row (from left): Jan Vining, Maura (O'Malley) McDonald, and Mary Beth Simons

Back Row (from left): Jim Ladner and Matt Feeney (Moreau Seminary, July 12, 2015)

Clockwise from left: Don McNeill, C.S.C.; Mary Beth (Simons) Ward; Brother Ricardo Palacio, C.F.C.; Jan Vining; Maura (O'Malley) McDonald; Steve Podry; Mary Ann Roemer; Don Fetters, C.S.C.; Matt Feeney; and Jim Ladner (South Bend, Indiana, July 11, 2015)

showcased student acoustic music, mostly covers of the mellow singer/
songwriter artists of that era. While some students frequented the
under-aged off-campus bars, my friends and I stayed on campus and
made music. We loved the Nazz.

During one of my late-night visits to the Nazz in the fall of my
senior year, I came across a closed office located on a stairwell landing
in LaFortune. I asked one of my friends what it was, and she told me
it was a resource center for students exploring postgraduate volunteer
opportunities. I went back to that stairwell landing the following week
and entered a small office. It smelled of freshly brewed coffee and
hummed with good conversation. There I met Mary Ann Roemer,
who was an unusually good listener, irreverent, and completely
disarming. I told her I was thinking about a year of volunteer service
after graduation (I'm not sure I had told that to anyone at that point).

Mary Ann gave me several brochures describing various programs,
including the Holy Cross Associates. Mary Ann explained that the
Congregation of Holy Cross had created this new program for recent
college graduates to encourage lay ministry and foster a stronger bond
between Holy Cross and the laity. She said that the HCA program was
founded on four core "pillars": service, simple lifestyle, community, and
spirituality. Those accepted into the domestic program would serve a
one-year commitment in Portland, Oregon, or Phoenix, Arizona.

Over the next few weeks I applied to and was accepted into
various law schools, including Notre Dame. I spoke to my parents
about the HCA program during Christmas break in late 1978.
They were both very supportive of whatever I chose to do, whether
law school or the HCA program. Years later my mom told me that
my dad couldn't understand why I didn't go straight to law school
after graduation. That would have been his choice, one he would
have easily made. But he did what good dads do and supported my
dreams, not his. He kept his mouth shut.

I was accepted into the Holy Cross Associates program in early 1979.

SELECTED LIFE LESSONS

On Thursday, July 26, 1979, I knew I was exactly where God intended me to be. I was on a plane traveling from St. Louis to Colorado Springs. My Notre Dame classmate Margaret Simkovsky, who had also been accepted into the HCA program, met me at the Colorado Springs airport. We attended a Judy Collins concert at Red Rocks, a beautiful outdoor amphitheater, on Saturday, July 28. Early the next week we began a retreat at the Holy Cross novitiate in Cascade, Colorado, with the other new Holy Cross Associates. Margaret went to Portland, and I drove to Phoenix with my HCA community members: Jim Ladner, Maura O'Malley, Mary Beth Simons, and Jan Vining.

My HCA experience taught me many life lessons, including the following five.

1. BE A TEACHER. As I approached my Notre Dame graduation, I worried about teaching in the fall without any training. I went to Fr. Gene's living room one night and asked him for teaching advice. He slumped back in his La-Z-Boy recliner, ran his left hand through his white hair, and then stroked his beard with his right hand. He sat quietly for what seemed an eternity. I remember thinking how old he looked at that moment and feeling vaguely sorry that I had put him on the spot.

Then, without saying a word, he began to rise from his chair and, while doing so, puffed out his chest, threw back his shoulders, and raised his chin. When he was fully standing, straight as a pin, he looked downright majestic. Before my eyes, Fr. Gene transformed from a tired, slouching old man into the poised, elegant professor who had stood before me in class so many times. Then he slowly turned his head toward me.

"Be a teacher," he said dramatically.

That's all Fr. Gene said. That's all he *needed* to say. Fr. Gene was not going to educate me on "teaching methods." God had apparently reserved that job for Sr. Etienne, who you will meet shortly. Rather, Fr. Gene went to the "bearing" of being a good teacher. First, and perhaps foremost, you must carry yourself like a teacher. Becoming a good teacher will hopefully follow, but without first "being" a teacher, that is much less likely to happen.

I used that advice with good success in the classroom, and I have used that advice with good success in life. Throughout our long careers as lawyers, there are some days when Michele and I simply want to crawl into bed and pull the covers over our heads. Invoking Fr. Gene's words, one of us will say to the other, "It's time to be a lawyer." I know that deciding to carry myself a certain way on the outside will oftentimes transform me on the inside. Kurt Vonnegut Jr. wrote, "We are what we pretend to be, so we must be careful about what we pretend to be."[104] Vonnegut's words were a warning; Fr. Gene's words ("be a teacher") are a compass.

2. BE FIRM, FAIR, AND CONSISTENT. Although Fr. Gene gave me solid advice about teacher bearing, I still lacked the *substance* of being a good teacher. So, during the summer of 1979 I checked out books from the local library about teaching in inner-city Catholic schools. The books I chose were all written in the late 1960s, and they had a consistent theme: your students come from disadvantaged backgrounds; what they need from you, as their teacher, is a kind, accepting friend who will gently guide them to life's truths. That made sense to me. One author explained a preferred approach to teaching religion class: first, light a candle; then, ask all of the children to sit down on a rug (preferably of the "shag" variety), play a Cat Stevens song to calm everyone down, and remind them that they're about to enter a sacred time and space. I loved Cat Stevens, so, again, this made sense to me.

---

104 Kurt Vonnegut, *Mother Night* (New York: Delta Trade Paperbacks, 1999).

I arrived at St. Matthew in mid-August 1979 met the principal, Sr. Etienne McDonald, BVM, and began teacher "in-service" meetings before school began. During breaks, Sr. Etienne listened patiently while I explained my enlightened teaching philosophy. At that point in her life, she had taught grade school for more than forty years, but I wanted to make sure she appreciated my preparation and confidence. At one point, just to be polite, I asked Sr. Etienne whether she had any advice for me.

"I really don't have any advice," Sr. Etienne said, "but I do have an observation."

"I'm very interested in your observation, Sister," I said.

"OK," she replied. "A weak woman teacher is a *sad* thing." She seemed to draw out the word "sad." "The children take control of the classroom, the teacher can't regain control, and for the entire year it's a miserable experience for both the teacher and the students."

I listened, somewhat puzzled, and she continued.

"On the other hand," she said, "a weak *man* teacher is"—and here she paused for dramatic effect—"pathetic."

Her observation had the desired effect. It was time to put aside the candles and Cat Stevens. School was starting in three days. It was time to be scared. It was time to listen.

"Sister, what do you suggest I do?" I asked, with a touch of desperation in my voice.

"Well," she said, "the first thing I would do is throw away all of those books you've been reading. Based on what you're telling me, I question whether the authors have ever set foot in a classroom." Then she looked at me in a steely-eyed, "nun-in-charge" way. "Maybe you've heard the old saying that teachers should not smile before Halloween. In this school, I wouldn't smile before Christmas. And above all," she added, "be firm, fair, and consistent."

"Firm, fair, and consistent." The words hung in the air like Sr. Etienne had painted them with a mystical nun brush. They had a solid ring of truth. I took Sr. Etienne's advice in all respects, except that I could not wait until Christmas to smile—I smiled on Halloween. I was wrong in doing so, of course; I spent much of the rest of the year trying to keep a lid on the class. I managed to do so, but I spent far much more energy than I otherwise would have.

But that "firm, fair, and consistent" advice remained with me throughout the year as my North Star. And that advice followed me into parenthood and into my professional life, both as a lawyer and as a law firm leader. Thank you, Sr. Etienne, for helping me at St. Matthew and throughout my life. May you rest in peace.

3. RESPECT MARY BETH'S SPONGES. It's easy to be judgmental when you're twenty-two. "Simple living" was one of the core pillars of the Holy Cross Associates program. My HCA community members and I pooled all of our salaries (everyone earned $4,500 that year except me—Sr. Etienne insisted that I take the "regular" St. Matthew salary of $6,300), and from these pooled funds we each received a $50 monthly stipend for personal expenses.

We spent several hours differentiating between "community" and "personal" expenses. After much reflection, prayer, and conversation, we concluded that community expenses included feminine products and beer. But things became more complicated when I helped put away groceries after Jan, Mary Beth, and Maura returned from their first grocery store trip. They had purchased all of the agreed-upon items, and all seemed right with the world. That is, until I discovered, at the bottom of one of the bags, name-brand scouring sponges that cost almost $3.

Mustering all of the conflict resolution skills that Mary Ann Roemer had taught us during the Cascade retreat, I calmly said to the three shoppers, "When you purchase name-brand scouring sponges that cost almost $3, it makes me feel wasteful." Everyone stopped dead in their tracks and turned toward me. Mary Beth looked both hurt and angry. "What had I done wrong?" I asked myself. "Hadn't I properly used an 'I feel' statement to express my point of view?" After all, I wasn't judging anyone, at least not overtly. I was simply telling my community members how I "felt."

Mary Beth was the first to speak. "When I was growing up, my family used this brand of sponge every night to clean the dishes. It's important to me that I have these sponges this year." Mary Beth had me at "family." Nothing about families is particularly rational. That goes double for large Irish Catholic families like mine. Mary Beth's sponge was like a Linus blanket, albeit an expensive one. It tied her in some inexplicable but meaningful way to her family. I knew right then and there that I needed to measure "simple living" with a flexible yardstick. To me, the sponges were extravagant; to Mary Beth, they were essential. When I find myself trying to understand how a person or family decides to spend their time or money on something that makes no sense to me, I often think of Mary Beth's sponges. When someone tries to understand why my family or I decide to spend our time or money in a certain way, I can only hope they once had a Mary Beth in their life.

4. BEWARE OF NUNS BEARING RULERS. Sr. Elaine taught sixth-, seventh-, and eighth-grade math in the classroom next to mine. The first time I entered her classroom, I felt like I was walking into a church. The room was silent, the children were doing their work, and Sr. Elaine sat on a stool with a math book in her lap, fully in command. She was four foot ten, heavy set, had a "bowl" haircut that made her gray hair look like a badly designed hat, and sported a perpetual sneer that would have made Elvis proud. She had a habit of correcting students by starting with "Look here, Buster!" She was the teacher the students deathly feared, she was the teacher whose students scored well above the local and national norms on standardized math tests and earned their way into high schools in the "nice" part of town, and she was the teacher students visited to thank long after they graduated. I wondered how she did it.

About two weeks into the school year, my seventh-grade students returned to my classroom following Sr. Elaine's math class. They were unusually quiet and seemed mildly traumatized. I was still in my "no smile" mode, so I asked forcefully, "What's going on here?"

Ida Mendoza dutifully raised her hand. "Sr. Elaine hit Floyd with a ruler. She hit him so hard that the ruler broke and slammed against the wall." I looked around the room. All of the other children, including Floyd, were nodding in agreement. Floyd was a small, hyperactive African American boy who frequently went off task. Today he would probably be diagnosed with attention deficit disorder, medicated, and considered a compliant, model student. When lunchtime came, I marched righteously across 21st Avenue to the convent, where the nuns were eating lunch. I made a beeline for the empty seat next to Sr. Elaine.

"I understand you had a problem with Floyd today," I said flatly, my sense of moral indignation hanging in the air.

Sr. Elaine put down her sandwich and turned to me.

"What?" she said, looking puzzled.

"Floyd—the broken ruler!" I blurted out.

Sr. Lillian, who taught second grade, turned to the sixth-grade teacher, Sr. Joy, and giggled. "It looks like Floyd got the ruler," Sr. Lillian said, which made all the nuns laugh, especially Sr. Elaine.

I could feel my blood boiling. Everything that was ever said about sadistic nuns must be true, I thought, as Sr. Elaine cackled through her sneer.

Sr. Elaine abruptly turned to me. "Look here, Buster!" she barked at me while reaching into her purse. She pulled out a ruler—I assumed THE ruler—but it wasn't broken. She tapped it on the table, and it snapped in two. The nuns laughed.

"Floyd drew the short straw this year," Sr. Elaine said after she stopped laughing. "I've had this ruler for over thirty years. I was about to throw it away after it broke in the 1940s, but then I had an idea. Rather than waste the ruler, I glued it back together. Every school year since I've given one of my students a swat on the seat. That breaks the ruler and scares the hell out of my students. And then they learn for the rest of the year." The nuns laughed again. Sr. Joy slapped the table.

I sat there dumbfounded. I didn't know whether to curse at Sr. Elaine or give her a standing ovation. I'm *still* not sure what to do, and I've had thirty-seven years to think about it. But I do know this: her students *did* learn that year.

5. LEARN HOW TO HUG. I grew up in a family that wasn't very physically or emotionally demonstrative. When I moved to Phoenix to begin my HCA year, I found myself living with four other people who had very different families than mine in this respect. Part of our HCA experience involved building a spiritual community. Early in the HCA year, Fr. Don Fetters, C.S.C., our HCA local director, was celebrating Mass in our apartment. It was time for the "sign of peace." In a parish setting, this is easy. You simply hold out your hand to the person next to you (often a stranger), avert your eyes, and mumble "peace be with you." In our apartment setting, however, the expectation was quite different. The only acceptable sign of peace was a hug.

Before then, I had never considered whether I was a "good hugger" or a "bad hugger." But the young women in my community quickly concluded that I fell in the latter category. "Jesus, Feeney!" Mary Beth exclaimed, "Who taught you how to hug?" So, Mary Beth, Jan, and Maura gave me hugging lessons. I learned to hug. More importantly, I learned to listen to and live with strong women, so much so that I married one. Hugging well is a metaphor for communicating well. Communicating well is the key to building strong relationships. Building strong relationships is essential to a happy life, both professionally and personally. Mary Beth, Jan, and Maura: I owe you another good hug.

SERVICE TO THE POOR

I moved into my HCA year with a résumé devoid of service and a soul yearning for a connection with the divine, nurtured by the good people I had encountered at Notre Dame. I dived into the deep end of the service pool during my HCA year by teaching at St. Matthew. I grew during that year, so much so that I seriously considered remaining at St. Matthew after my HCA year. As I sorted through the decision to either remain at St. Matthew or return to Notre Dame for law school, St. Paul's famous epistle to the Corinthians came to mind:

> If I speak in human and angelic tongues, but do not have love, I am a resounding gong or a clanging cymbal.[105]

I realized that, although I felt I was "good" at teaching and was making a positive difference in children's lives, I did not love teaching. It was time to move on. I have had similar experiences in my life, whether serving on charitable boards or becoming involved in matters because "it's the right thing to do." If I find myself going through the motions or feel a lack of joy or personal commitment, even if the "cause" is objectively a good one, I look for a way to step back from the activity.

Professor G. Robert Blakey was a long-time, well-respected Notre Dame Law School professor. I met Michele in Professor Blakey's Criminal Law class, which was the first class of our law school career. Professor Blakey was bright, intimidating, and demanding. And, just as Sr. Elaine's students loved her class, I loved Professor Blakey's class.

At the start of my third year of law school, as I was considering what to do after graduation, I went to Professor Blakey's office.

"Professor," I said, "I'm seriously considering an offer from a Phoenix law firm that feels like a very good fit for me. I love the

---

105 First Corinthians 13:1, *The Catholic Study Bible,* second edition (New York: Oxford University Press, 2011).

people there, I love Phoenix, and Michele is open to moving there with me."

"So what's the problem?" he asked.

"I feel like I should be doing something more altruistic, more service-focused, maybe like working for legal aid or something like that."

Professor Blakey looked at me carefully. "It sounds to me like you *think* that's something you should do but perhaps don't want to do."

I sat there silently, hearing St. Paul's clanging cymbal, not knowing what to say.

"You know," Professor Blakey said, "I firmly believe attorneys can make the same or even more of a difference working in the Exxon law department or in a large law firm than they can make in a legal aid clinic. A lawyer of conscience can make a meaningful difference anywhere. Trust me, if you become a good lawyer, you will have plenty of opportunities to do so."

That was not the answer I expected, but it was the answer I needed to hear. I wanted to go to Snell & Wilmer. I wanted to become a good lawyer. And I needed to believe that I would still have the chance to make a positive difference in the world.

Thirty-three years have passed since I graduated from Notre Dame Law School. I remain at Snell & Wilmer. All of those years I have been a corporate lawyer, something I never would have imagined doing. I have tried to make a positive difference, and, in some respects, I have succeeded.

First, let me start with my family. I believe Michele and I have raised (and continue to raise) five loving and compassionate souls. If I do nothing else in my life, that alone will be enough for me. I have tried to be a good husband and father and was fortunate to have married someone who tries to be a good wife and mother. Michele and I began our relationship drinking coffee together every morning before working on a research project for Professor Blakey during the summer of 1981, between our first and second years of law school. During our marriage we begin each day drinking coffee together, sometimes over the telephone when one of us is traveling. When people ask me how we have managed to stay married so long, my answer always includes "good coffee, good communication, and good confrontation." Perhaps the last piece of my answer has its roots in the conflict resolution skills Mary Ann Roemer taught the incoming Holy Cross Associates in Cascade, Colorado ("You need to learn how to fight fairly").

The window in my first Snell & Wilmer office faced directly west. From the twenty-ninth floor I could see St. Matthew twenty blocks away. It was as if God were reminding me not to forget, to keep my heart open to new ways to make a difference. My day-to-day work provides me with opportunities to do so. One of my early Snell & Wilmer mentors told me that clients *want* their lawyers to tell them when they're going astray. That has been my experience. The vast majority of people want to do the right thing, in business or otherwise.

In 1984, two Holy Cross priests, Mike Baxter and John Fitzgerald ("Fitz"), appeared at my office to tell me about their plan to establish a Catholic Worker house of hospitality for the poor, which they were going to call Andre House, after Brother (now Saint) Andre Bessette, a Holy Cross brother. I met Mike in a fiction writing class at Notre Dame. When I was a law student at Notre Dame in the early 1980s, I helped Fitz administer the HCA program. Fitz and Mike were very pastoral priests, but neither would place organizational skills high on their list of strengths. Mike and Fitz asked me to review the Andre House lease.

That evening, in violation of all client confidentiality rules, I told Michele about my meeting with Mike and Fitz. I told her that if they succeeded with Andre House, it would have to be the Holy Spirit's work, because their vision seemed much larger than their collective ability to pull it off. And it was. But like all good visions firmly rooted in justice and diligently and sincerely pursued, their vision of Andre House attracted like-minded souls. And those people attracted others. Well over thirty years later, Andre House is thriving under the leadership of yet another remarkable Holy Cross priest, Fr. Tom Doyle.

Mike Baxter returned to my office in 1988 and said the Andre House community was exploring the idea of a job service for the homeless. I no longer doubted Mike's ability to pull off anything. I formed the St. Joseph Worker Job Service (SJW) as a new business entity, and Mike asked me to join the board, which I willingly did. I have remained associated with SJW for almost thirty years, and it remains a charitable focus of the Feeney family. For the past nine years, my acoustic musical group, feeney/winthrop, has performed an annual concert at a local girls' Catholic high school to benefit SJW. To date, these concerts have raised more than $300,000 to support SJW's good work.

The feeney/winthrop group consists of Larry Winthrop and his wife, Pat; my sister, Kathleen; Gerry Garcia (who played bass in a Notre Dame band with me in the 1970s); Luke Holton, a former Phoenix neighbor and a long-time friend; and me. Larry was a partner of mine at Snell & Wilmer in the late 1980s, and we cochaired the firm's pro bono committee. We presented a pro bono policy to firm management that provided attorneys with full "billable hour" credit if they performed legal services for the poor. The firm adopted that policy, one of the first of its kind in the nation. Since that time, Snell & Wilmer attorneys have provided tens of thousands of pro bono hours to the poor.

I say these things not to boast. Rather, I say them to demonstrate that I believe Professor Blakey was right. I believe even a corporate lawyer in a big law firm can do a decent amount of good work for the poor if he or she is open to doing so.

If I have one criticism of the HCA program, at least in its early years, it's that the program may have failed to recognize that most of its alumni will ultimately pursue more traditional occupations after they complete their HCA year. I knew several HCA alumni who felt they had somehow failed or "sold out" because they did not remain in an inner-city school or at a food bank following their HCA year. The HCA program may not have paid enough attention to the vast majority of alumni who went into more "mainstream" jobs. Perhaps the program could have used a Professor Blakey.

COLLABORATION WITH THE CONGREGATION OF HOLY CROSS—COMPANIONS ON MISSION

I was proud to be a Holy Cross Associate because, at least in my mind, it meant that I was part of Holy Cross's mission of being educators in the faith "with a preferential option for the poor."[106] My involvement with Andre House and St. Joseph the Worker Job Service and my deep commitment to Notre Dame flow from my connection to Holy Cross.

Unfortunately, it does not appear the HCA program ever cultivated, or attempted to connect, the Holy Cross Associate alumni in any meaningful and sustained way. Hundreds, if not thousands, of young people were Holy Cross Associates from the late 1970s through the early 2000s. I am sure that many HCAs completed their year of service feeling a deep connection to Holy Cross. But most relationships die without cultivation.

For several years during the 1990s, Fr. Don McNeill led weekend gatherings of laypeople with ties to Holy Cross, including former Holy Cross Associates and their families, in Deer Park, Maryland, the site of a Holy Cross summer residence. The invitation letter for the 1998 "Deer Park Gathering" described the weekend as an

---

106 Constitution of the Congregation of Holy Cross, 2:12.

opportunity "to discuss the challenges of living and working as a Christian in the church and in the world today."

Those weekends were intense and wonderful and deepened my connection to Holy Cross. Years later I realized that Don's instincts told him at the time of the Deer Park Gatherings that the Holy Cross Associates program needed to build connections among its alumni to survive. I remember him laughing during one of those weekends when he told me he needed to "resist the McNeill-ian urge to convert every good experience [like the Deer Park Gatherings] into a program." Giving rise to Don's comment was his idea that perhaps the Deer Park Gatherings (or something like them) could be institutionalized in a program called "Companions on Mission." Whether or not Don's idea was a good one from a programmatic perspective, Don coined a beautiful title for that never-to-be program.

The 2006 Provincial Chapter of the Congregation of Holy Cross Indiana Province terminated the Holy Cross Associates program, effective following the 2007–2008 year, because "times have changed and it is not clear that the Holy Cross Associates program can or should continue in its present form."[107] The chapter report stated that similar programs were proliferating, HCA applications were down, and that "it is possible that the Holy Cross Associates as it is currently constituted has outgrown its usefulness."[108] The HCA alumni were not immediately informed of the program's termination, and many, including me, were saddened by this decision.

On July 10–12, 2015, all of my former HCA housemates from Phoenix gathered at Notre Dame for the thirty-fifth anniversary of the completion of our HCA year. Joining us were Brother Ricardo Palacio, a Christian brother who taught with me at St. Matthew, and Steve Podry, my Notre Dame roommate who bicycled across the

---

107 Proceedings of the Provincial Chapter, Congregation of the Holy Cross (2006), Recommendation 39.
108 Ibid.

United States during our HCA year and spent several weeks with us in Phoenix.

Through the good graces of our Notre Dame classmate, Fr. Jim McDonald, C.S.C., we stayed at Moreau Seminary on the Notre Dame campus, the same place where we were given our housing assignments in May 1979. It marked the first time all of us had been together since Jan's wedding in 1983. The bonds forged during our HCA year brought us to a place of trust and vulnerability that resulted in deeply personal discussions about our life experiences. The weekend ended with hugs—I made sure that I hugged Mary Beth well. I will never forget that weekend.

Next to Moreau Seminary lies Holy Cross House. As fate—or God's hand—would have it, Fr. Don Fetters, our HCA Phoenix local director, was there recovering from an illness. Fr. Don McNeill was also living there. Mary Ann Roemer, the person who introduced me to the Holy Cross Associates, drove down from her home near Lake Michigan. After looking "back" on our shared history with laughter, nostalgia, and gratitude, we looked "forward" and wondered (some would say, "schemed") about how Holy Cross could revive the HCA program or something like it.

I don't have many things on my "bucket list," but here is one: to resurrect the Holy Cross Associates program. I want to do so for future college graduates who are, and will be, inspired by Holy Cross and who will want to devote a year or two of service side by side with Holy Cross. Perhaps that service will lead to a lifetime collaborative relationship with Holy Cross, as it has done for me, a Companion on Mission.

CHAPTER 7

Holy Cross Associates in the United States: Sociological Insights into Formation in Intentional Community[109]

Mary Ellen Konieczny

INTRODUCTION

*H*eading to Colorado Springs for orientation with other incoming Holy Cross Associates (HCA) in the summer of 1981, it never occurred to me that my housemates and I would be "formed" as we lived together in community that year. Like others in our cohort, I was newly graduated from Notre Dame and ready to take the next step in a journey into adulthood. Attracted by a desire for service—and in my case, a year to discern whether a life of service within the Catholic Church was for me—my placement in a Portland parish was foremost in my mind. The religious basis of the program felt natural to me, since my desire to be of service to others had grown within me along with my faith. I looked forward optimistically to getting to know my housemates and figuring out what it meant to live simply in community. I also hoped that the experiences of the

---

109 Thank you to Fr. Christopher Kuhn and Mrs. Deborah Buzzard at the Congregation of Holy Cross US Province Archives Center, who graciously facilitated my review and use of documents related to the Holy Cross Associates program.

year would help me to grow out of the awkwardness of my youth, at least a little bit. But I really had no idea how that might happen.

Certainly, even if I had been expecting it, I would have had very little sense of what formation was. Nor did I know what it would mean for my life trajectory. So, as we arrived in Colorado Springs for orientation, I had no real understanding or awareness of the most central experience of the Associate year—the formation that would take place among and within us as we lived in intentional community.

Thinking back on my ignorance, I wondered: Was my experience common, or had I been just dense or naive? Did incoming Associates through the years understand and desire the experience of formation in lay community? Perhaps most important, how did this formation in intentional community happen, and did experiences of formation differ over time? What did Associates' formation produce in their lives?

My answers to these questions are no doubt inflected by my own experiences past and present. They are informed by discussions I have had with my fellow Associates in the many years since I served and also by the written reflections of Associates sampled from archived newsletters over the twenty-eight years of the program. Orientation materials and other documents related to the administration of the program drawn from the Congregation of Holy Cross archives provided a context for how those who guided us during the HCA year thought about and prepared to form Associates in intentional lay community.

Perusing these documents joyfully animated my memories. But more importantly, they revealed patterns of experience and action among Holy Cross Associates over the arc of the program's history. Their musings, both in the midst of and after the volunteer year, give us insight into what it meant to be formed as an Associate living in an intentional lay community. These reflections, together with letters, notes, and reports of program and site directors, show how the four "pillars" of the program—community, prayer and spirituality, simple lifestyle, and service—were part of a new and developing understanding of the vocation of Catholic laity. Moreover, remembrances of alumni reveal how the program's formative effects endured in their lives in compelling and important ways. And while their concerns changed in a couple of distinct ways with new generations' experiences and challenges, the lasting outcomes of Associates' formation have remained constant over the years.

MOTIVATION AND MISSION

Those of us applying to the Holy Cross Associates as seniors at Notre Dame in 1980–1981 knew about the program largely through faith-based service organizations on campus such as the Council for the International Lay Apostolate (CILA) and campus ministry and through friends involved in service learning. The Associates were new then: the first community had been established in Portland, Oregon, only two years prior in 1978. But the program was growing quickly. By 1981 there were already two other domestic program sites— Hayward, California, and Phoenix, Arizona—and international sites in Santiago, Chile, and Nairobi, Kenya. When we arrived at Colorado Springs for our orientation, we knew that we were embarking on a year of volunteer service and community living where we would share prayer and live simply, but few of us knew the details of the program's founding. I also remember thinking later that year that even upon the conclusion of orientation as we headed to our sites, many of us (including me) had little idea of what we had gotten ourselves into.

It was only long after my Associates year that I came to appreciate how the history and foundation of the Holy Cross Associates and the motivations and vision of those who animated it had helped to structure and facilitate our work and community life during that year in Portland. An HCA newsletter article written during the twenty-fifth anniversary year of the program in 2003 tells the story of its founding

briefly but in a revealing way. It describes the original intent of the
founding of the Holy Cross Associates as arising out of a 1977 conversation between Fr. Tim Scully, C.S.C. (then a seminarian), and Fr. Jerry
Wilson, C.S.C., who was then on the staff of Moreau Seminary. They
wanted to tap "the energy, faith, goodwill, and availability of recent
college graduates"[110] in an effort similar to the Peace Corps or the Jesuit
Volunteers. But they wanted to create something that was more than
just a volunteer service program. They envisioned "a program which
would combine elements particularly fitted to [their] own Holy Cross
tradition and charism which would draw these young people into a
particular relationship with the Holy Cross community."[111] Apparently,
they moved quickly with the idea, since the inaugural Associates community in Portland, Oregon, was established a year later.

Two things about this account are striking. The first is the clarity
and practicality of this vision. These Holy Cross religious recognized
not only the virtue in responding to a motivating idealism among
many emerging adults but also the fact that recent college graduates
are at a particularly available time in the life course. It is a very good
time of life to spend a year in volunteer service. Of course, there were
other volunteer programs that recognized this as well. But that those
who fashioned the Associates would see the opportunity is no surprise,
since to recognize and seize favorable circumstances in building God's
kingdom are very much in the spirit of the Holy Cross tradition.

The second is their intention to imbue the program with elements
of the congregation's charism—which other faith-based programs
such as the Jesuit Volunteers do as well—but in so doing also to draw
Associates into a definite relationship with the congregation. Elements
of the congregation's charism are evident in the pillars of the program
and in the ways in which they are lived out but perhaps no element
more so than the ways in which Associates were encouraged to form

110 "Beginnings," *The Anchor*, vol. III, no. 1 (Spring 2003), US Province Archives Center (USPAC).
111 Ibid.

relationships with one another in community. And this was modeled in the warm welcome of the congregation's communities at many of the program's sites. I believe these patterns of relationship to be a reflection of the guiding image initially envisioned by the congregation's founder, Fr. Basil Moreau, C.S.C., for his religious communities Holy Cross priests, brothers, and sisters—that of a family.

At the same time, the vision that connected the charism of Holy Cross to the founding and structuring of the Holy Cross Associates also included an awareness of its relationship to the broader Catholic Church. In this vision, the Associates represented one response to the emerging "signs of the times" enunciated at Vatican II and so widely discussed during the period of implementation of its reforms.

On the occasion of the associates' tenth anniversary in 1988, Fr. Richard V. Warner, C.S.C., wrote that, from its beginnings, the Associates "were not something completely new." Rather, they were a part of "a long standing Holy Cross tradition . . . Our program stands on broad shoulders, and each succeeding generation of Holy Cross Associates adds to this long tradition."[112] This tradition is not only a familial one but also one that draws attention to the congregation's work in recognizing and supporting an empowered laity. From the middle decades of the twentieth century onward, Warner explains, friends of Notre Dame and Holy Cross religious have worked with, acknowledged, and encouraged the unique vocations of laypeople in the modern world. This happened first with Catholic Action groups. He recognizes Fr. Louis Putz, a Chicago priest inspired by Catholic Action's founder, Belgian Cardinal Joseph Cardijn, as one of these collaborators; he brought a Young Christian Students group to Notre Dame. He also names Fr. Marcos McGrath, C.S.C. (later Archbishop of Panama), who began social action and reflection groups in Santiago, Chile, as another. And similarly, he includes the work of

---

112 "From Richard V. Warner, CSC," *Holy Cross Associates Newsletter* (August 1988), USPAC.

Fr. Don McNeill, C.S.C., in this trajectory, citing the many experiential learning and service programs Padre Don animated and the eventual founding of Notre Dame's Center for Social Concerns. In this work, Warner proudly observes, Holy Cross developed "an approach to lay ministry and spirituality which influenced the course of their [participants'] lives."[113]

This history helps us to understand why the Holy Cross Associates formed its members in intentional lay community as it did. The emphasis on lay formation comes from the experience of Holy Cross religious with Catholic Action and their openness to collaboration and partnership with laity. And their charism, and especially Fr. Moreau's vision of Holy Cross as a family, created a particularly intimate understanding of what it meant to be formed in Associate community. We can see this underlying logic in participants' experiences of the four pillars and how they were lived out in common during the Associate year.

INTENTIONAL COMMUNITY AND THE FOUR PILLARS

Associates over the years have come to the program for a number of different reasons. For some, it was a place to figure out the next step in their lives. For others, it was a way to take a break in their educational and career trajectory with a "gap" year. For still others, they came because friends had done it and found it fulfilling. Along with these motivations, many were attracted by one or more of the objectives of the program, which as the program matured came to be called the "four pillars": community, service, simple living, and prayer and spirituality.

---

113 Ibid.

Among these pillars, community played a special role in Associates' formation. This is so because it was in community not only where relationships between members were created and deepened but also where Associates' experiences of the four pillars were ultimately integrated into their common life and each member's sense of self. In other words, community was where members shared not only life but also faith, as they reflected upon each of the pillars with one another. This process is at the heart of how formation happened among Holy Cross Associates.

Over the years, Associates have written in strikingly similar ways about the problems, challenges, lighter moments, and unexpected joys of living the four pillars. In their words, presented and discussed in what follows, we glimpse the common experiences that contributed to Associates' formation in intentional community. Since, in a sense, community bookends the other pillars as the place where formation begins and comes to fullness, this begins with Associates' experiences of living in community and returns to community again in the following section to draw out what these experiences reveal about how we were formed as Holy Cross Associates.

COMMUNITY

From the beginning of the Associate year, experiences of community living ran the gamut from disagreement and difficulties to support, appreciation, and joy. Previously, we had lived with our families and with roommates. But living with people we didn't know well in a structured way, one that required us to get to know and work with one another with some intimacy, was new for most of us. Schooled at orientation with tips and techniques for navigating interpersonal relationships and making a household work, before long we were figuring things out for ourselves. This happened as soon as we left orientation, or at least upon our arrival at the house in which we would live together. One Colorado group recounted their initial experience of trying to make decisions as a newly formed community this way:

> That evening, community decision making commenced. The topic at hand: who will sleep in what room? Group decisions involve weighing the pros and cons of all options. All the members and suggestions must be given equal attention. Quite often, painstaking hours are spent deliberating a particular issue. With these factors in mind, the drained Associates flipped a coin . . . Fortunately, as the days progressed, the group decision making process did as well . . .[114]

Decision making by consensus was the aim in Associate community—though not always realized. And there were many decisions to be made, especially at the start of the year. This brought Associate communities to an early awareness of differences among their members, as the Colorado house that had executed the coin flip recognized:

> It didn't take a long time to realize that this Associate house had been "lambasted with a bevy of motley personalities." In other words, after removing the SAT buzzwords correctly and/or incorrectly used, the house was "hit hard with a multitude of different personalities." What did this mean? The upcoming year was going to be a challenging one.[115]

---

114 Fran Fleming, "From Colorado," *Holy Cross Associates Newsletter* (October–November 1990), USPAC.
115 Ibid.

The inevitable "multitude of different personalities" was a challenge in Associate houses generally because of the closeness that living in community entailed. Although Associate communities commonly called their members "housemates," we weren't merely living with roommates. While we needed to work out the details of a household, this wasn't just a negotiation with acquaintances or a business relationship. Living in intentional community required an effort to develop relationships among ourselves that would be mutually and personally supportive. This was no small task. Many of us experienced community as a process of continuous work. Building community challenged each member practically and emotionally.

Despite this challenge—and also likely, in part, because of it—by midyear most groups were thoroughly enjoying life in community, at least much of the time. For example, one Associate wrote of midyear in the Brockton house:

> We have crossed the sixth month border . . . [and]
> learned how to turn life's simplest moments into the
> greatest pleasures. For example, during the past month,
> we have managed to conquer the city of Boston, survived
> the abominable Blizzard of '96, stayed fit the YMCA
> way, and enjoyed a few outings with our co-workers and
> community. Most important, we have learned to live fun
> lives on only $60 a month.[116]

Associate communities adventured together: they found ways to meet their common needs, responded to unexpected challenges, and recreated, all while getting to know a new city. These were some of the basic experiences of living in Associate community. Characteristically, communities usually did this with a healthy

---

116 Maria Mayola and Melissa Pinto, "From Massachusetts," *Holy Cross Associates Newsletter* (February 1996).

dose of humor. I don't remember being schooled in this during orientation, but it was a sort of wisdom that was common in Associate houses throughout the years. It came in handy, especially as we navigated some of the other objectives of the program, perhaps especially its requirement to live simply.

SIMPLE LIVING

Good-natured humor, along with a more serious awareness of deprivation and want throughout the world, was central to the experience of simple living at my Portland house. Coming into the program, I knew intellectually that many Catholics—some, like Dorothy Day, whom many of us found inspiring—saw a voluntary simple lifestyle as one lived in solidarity with the poor. Having come from a working-class household, I knew firsthand what it meant to do without. On entering the program, I took living simply for granted since I had always had to live that way. But I learned during that year what it meant to do so voluntarily, realizing that, as a new Notre Dame graduate (albeit a first-generation one) I was no longer a person without means or social advantage.

A simple lifestyle was thoroughly integrated into Associate community living by necessity. The structure of the program included funds for the household and small monthly personal stipends. It was up to us as a community to decide how to use household funds to meet the cost of meals and other expenses, and each individual was responsible for staying within the bounds of his or her small personal allowance. In so doing, the requirement to live simply begged us to reflect on its meaning—and especially its connection to an option for the poor—even as we carried out daily routines and made choices as seemingly insignificant as choices of meals or recreational activities. This theme permeates the newsletter reports from Associate houses over the years. They often referred to the nitty-gritty details of life, in "homemade Christmas presents, inexpensive camping trips, generic corn flakes, beans and rice on Wednesdays, one-dollar movies, one bathroom."[117] Many of these details are followed by questions of capacity and meaning, like, "Are we living simply? What does it mean to live like Christ?"[118]

Simple living was often grist for discussion, especially as an act of wanting to live in solidarity with the poor. This desire would often grow in Associates as they moved through the twin experiences of simplicity and service. Oftentimes newsletter entries written by Associates became extended reflections on simplicity and solidarity, understood in the light of faith. Octavio Martin's reflections express sentiments that many Associates would identify with:

> I question my dreams of the classic middle class lifestyle:
> a nice house with a white picket fence, a new car, two
> kids and a dog. I ask myself whether these comforts
> mean an escape from the reality of the world we serve, or
> perhaps a denial of the suffering of our fellow man . . .
> In spite of our differences, there is much we can learn
> from the poor and our dedication to a simple lifestyle,
> mainly in the sense of true dependence on the God that
> is responsible for all we give and receive . . . Through
> the act of living simply, I believe that Jesus is asking us
> to get a feel for our dependence on God and our need to
> be conscious of His presence in our daily lives.[119]

Simple living is understood here not only as an act of solidarity but also as a way for Associates, as socially advantaged adults, to

---

117 Cecilia Bryer, "It's Simple," *Holy Cross Associates Newsletter* (February–March 1990), USPAC.
118 Ibid.
119 Octavio Martin, "A Reflection on Simple Lifestyle," *The Anchor* (Winter 1999–2000), USPAC.

recognize that although we are able to depend on ourselves for many things in life, we need to learn dependence upon God. At the same time, Associates inevitably struggled with the fact that, although we lived simply to stand in solidarity with the poor, we never would be economically poor or challenged in the ways those we met in our placement were poor. Martin went on to say, "We can never really mimic the plight of those we serve because our circumstances are, and always will be, very different . . . It often seems to me pure vanity to compare our lives to those of the people we serve."[120]

And the damage done by social and economic inequality was often particularly obvious in our service placements, where these realities were daily and concrete and all around us.

SERVICE

Although many and diverse reasons had attracted Associates to the program, service was the most obvious aspect of the program to newcomers and, for many, also the most familiar. It was also often the most consuming, the most challenging, and, ironically, the most unfamiliar—as we waded into responsibilities that tested our characters and ways of doing things, humbled us, and challenged us in ways that fostered growth. HCA service placements were varied: we worked with the homeless, the mentally and physically challenged, the abused, the elderly, and the young; we worked in schools, social service agencies, parishes, and other religious organizations. Newsletters over the years are filled with accounts of all of the pillars of the program but none more than stories of experiences of service, many like this one:

---

120 Ibid.

Casework at the Center for the Homeless is simply
indescribable . . . The social diversity of the guests
holds no limits. One mentally ill guest can describe to
you his journeys to other planets. Many alcoholics use
the Center as shelter for their sober eves. Yesterday, I
chatted a while with a man holding a bachelor's degree
in political science who had consciously chosen to be
homeless for the past five years. Some guests have been
here since day one. Other guests are just temporarily
going through tough times. At any rate, they are all
education, spiritual inspiration, and even entertainment
at my fingertips daily. I am very grateful for this
opportunity and enjoying every minute of it.[121]

Our Associate placements brought us into daily contact with
people who experienced persistent and painful troubles that we did
not. Many of the problems we were enlisted to help ameliorate were
intertwined with social stigma and structural inequality. Although
we approached our responsibilities with youthful energy, many of us
often found ourselves encountering problems that seemed enormous
and feeling as if there was very little we could do to change things.
These experiences demanded venting and processing. Much of this,
of course, happened with our housemates and was interwoven into
our formation.

Sometimes Associates wrote about the emotions provoked by
these experiences for one another:

Looking back over my varied experiences with Holy
Cross Associates and with St. Vincent's Day Home
since I began eons ago in August, I have difficulty aptly

---

121 Dave Masciolek, "From Indiana," *Holy Cross Associates Newsletter* (October–November 1990),
USPAC.

summing up my feelings . . . Frustration has arisen in
several different arenas at many different levels, many
from which I never even suspected difficulties. At work,
my position has been so uncertain as to swing from one
of relatively few responsibilities to one of tremendous
and even overwhelming responsibilities and back again
to even fewer; changes which have left me confused and
with a sometimes sneaking suspicion that perhaps I am
not suited to the position or (gasp) have failed myself
or the children I so want to help. Logically, I know that
my problems arise primarily from inexperience.[122]

The experiences of our placements, though different depending
upon our responsibilities and where we served, were shared in many
ways—we experienced many of the same feelings, challenges, often a
sense of puzzlement, and sometimes similar joys as well. And we could
not help but bring them to prayer, alone and in common, to express
our own pain and wonderment, and to try to make sense of them.

PRAYER AND SPIRITUALITY

Prayer was an integral objective of the Associates' program and,
like the other pillars, was structured into the routines of Associates'
lives in community. There were several structures put in place in
the HCA program to facilitate ongoing communal prayer. Perhaps
most important was the expectation that Associates pray in common
regularly in their communities. In our house in Portland, while we
shared prayer at meals and other times, prayer—often including
Mass said by one of the Holy Cross priests from the University of

---

122 Chris Collins, "From California," *Holy Cross Associates Newsletter* (October–November 1990),
    USPAC.

Portland—was also a regular part of our community night each week. Associate houses also had other resources and invitations to pray as well. Some went to Sunday Mass weekly together; neighboring Holy Cross communities often invited Associate communities to join them in prayer on their community nights or at other times. And spiritual direction resources were offered and encouraged for individuals.

Prayer was central to our formation in the sense that it was often the foundation for integrating the experiences of the other three pillars. This aspect of prayer as one integrating element of formation in intentional community becomes evident in the newsletters in the ways in which it appears—usually not on its own, per se, but in discussions of how the other pillars, most often those of simple living and service, are linked to faith. But prayer also gets mentions by Associates in newsletter entries in its own right—especially around the liturgical seasons of Advent, Christmas, Lent, and Easter. At these times, prayer is a practice, often one that is felt as a taken-for-granted part of being Catholic. For example, "Easter was filled with a wonderful Stonehill mass and then a home-cooked Easter Brunch . . . The Lenten season was blessed with reflections by Rick Gribble, CSC, as well as no chocolate, no seconds when eating, no dating (by choice)."[123]

Sometimes these familiar Catholic rituals and prayers became infused with new experiences or new meanings. One of the accounts I found most touching was of an Associate's experience of preaching during a Way of the Cross procession on Good Friday that made its way through the streets of Colorado Springs. He recalls, "There I stood on the altar at the exit ramp captivated by the crowd's undivided attention . . . 'The 14th Station: Jesus' Resurrection.' With confidence I moved into the meat of my homily." He is speaking from memory. He launches into the first several sentences of his speech and then pauses, frozen in embarrassment and, he says, "disgusted" with himself. Mortified and

---

123 Greg Martin, "From Massachusetts," *Holy Cross Associates Newsletter* (April 1996), USPAC.

weighing his options, he goes to find the text copy of his speech, begins again, and speaks until he completes it. He says about the experience:

> God was speaking truth to me in the midst of my shame. This became evident as I placed myself in the context of the day's recurrent themes: death and resurrection . . . While trying to lead a crowd in an experience of Christ's Resurrection, I encountered my very own death to myself. It is precisely here that I think God shared His wisdom with me. Even though my intention was to become more holy by serving God as an evangelist, I discovered that even there my ego had some say . . . Humility and perhaps humiliation, in my case, precedes and is necessary for new life.[124]

Reflections like this one were most common not when talking about the experience of prayer itself, as this one does, but rather when Associates were reflecting upon the other pillars and their ongoing experiences of the volunteer year. These reflections reveal some of the visible results of formation. As we see next, they testify to the ways in which not only prayer but also simple living and service became thoroughly grounded in our lives in intentional communities, constituted in formation and often experienced as the personal project of the Associate year.

LAY FORMATION IN INTENTIONAL COMMUNITY

Community was not only the site where Associates lived simply, engaged in prayer, shared service experiences, got to know one other, and found ways to have fun on a budget, but also a place where all of

---

124 Chris Peraro, "From Colorado," *Holy Cross Associates Newsletter* (May 1996), USPAC.

these aspects of Associate life came into conversation with each other. Moreover, as we shared these experiences, they touched us and made us vulnerable. In this way, community became a place of intimacy. This intimacy was anchored in a familial sense of community. And it was encouraged by local directors and spiritual advisors who were part of the Congregation of Holy Cross or closely associated with the congregation. Animated by the image of family on which the congregation was modeled, the intimate relationships that carried our formation often were inspired more through the attitudes of our directors than their words and more through action than reason.

We can view how this intimacy developed in Associate communities, especially in how participants wrote about their experiences of learning and growth in the program. These reflections reveal elements of the formation process as well as some of its outcomes. The centrality of intentional community in formation is evident as Associates wrote about how their communities provided space not only for important interpersonal interactions but also for reflection and, ultimately, personal growth. Some communities became aware of these effects of intentional community early on in the Associate year:

> My first three months as an Associate has inspired more
> serious spiritual reflection than I anticipated. Living
> a more simple and prayerful life in community while
> serving others has allowed me to examine myself, my
> lifestyle, and ambitions much more closely and honestly
> . . . The entire Hayward HCA community seems to
> be sharing a similar experience. The belief that being
> a Holy Cross Associate will not be just a one-year
> commitment but will be a life-long commitment to
> live a more simple and prayerful life has been expressed
> by different members of the community during mass,

community prayer, and personal discussions. The impact of our Holy Cross Associate experience is already being evidenced in the questioning and changing of post-Associate plans.[125]

As the months folded into one another, community members got to know each other better. Some verbalized vividly how, as the experience of community living deepened, they began to feel vulnerable in uncomfortable ways.

> There were times when it seemed overwhelming . . . and I wanted to pull myself away and bring myself back to a place that was familiar and comfortable to me. It felt like it would be easiest to close up, keep my feelings to myself, and protect myself from the challenges and struggles surrounding me . . . I wanted to avoid conflict (not that there's ever any of it in our house) within the community and not venture into that difficult and somewhat risky road. I wanted to keep my spirituality personal and private and out of the scrutiny of others. I wanted to get back to a place where I was comfortable with who I was and where I was going in life.[126]

As households grew in intimacy, members often also grew in affection for one another. Intimacy and affection created a safe place where individuals could feel their weaknesses more fully; there were so many new and challenging experiences in the Associate year, and they often came together overwhelmingly in community. This experience was uncomfortable, but it was also an invitation to growth. And so:

---

125 Bill Stoll, "From Hayward," *Holy Cross Associates Newsletter* (November 1987), USPAC.
126 Jason Woodward, "From Oregon," *Holy Cross Associates Newsletter* (February 1996), USPAC.

The main challenge became allowing myself to be
uncomfortable and taking the risk of receiving openly
all that was new and different, without knowing how it
would affect me. In order to learn from others I needed
to face the challenge of being present in the moment
and resist the temptation to look to the past or ahead to
the future . . . Facing this challenge has helped me to
feel like I'm really living and learning and has allowed
me to truly see God working in my life.[127]

As Associates, we experienced vulnerability in community that
not only invited us to grow but also allowed us to share and come to
terms with our experiences of service and what that meant for our
lives beyond the Associate year. Jamie Loftus, one of my Portland
housemates, described his experience of learning at his placement that
"for all of us, being our truest selves is being for others."[128] But the full
weight of that realization happened in community and happened for
each of us as we came to awareness of this insight together. He explains:

This discernment took place alone as well as in
community. We laughed, we cried, we talked, we prayed,
but most of all, we gave each other a sense of mission
and identity—service to others. It was impossible to
separate volunteering from Church ministry in our
house in Portland. Whether through joy or suffering,
ministry encouraged us to orient ourselves to the other.
Ministry asked us to be ourselves, with our limits and
our weaknesses. We cannot be all things to all people,
only fully ourselves.[129]

---

127 Ibid.
128 "How Does a Volunteer Program Change One's Life?" Report on the Holy Cross Associates
    program, 1990. USPAC.
129 Ibid.

Jamie's words reveal the profound sense of intimacy in our Portland house—the sense of connection that formed in us a common "sense of mission and identity." It was a common identity that allowed us—and drew out of us—a rounded self, which encompassed our strengths and patiently bore our weaknesses. This "true self" grew in each of us in relationship with each other. I experienced this keenly as I, an inveterate perfectionist, was encouraged to be more patient with my weaknesses as my housemates bore patiently with me.

Living simply in solidarity with the poor, prayer, and service ultimately formed us, in and with the help of our communities, into people who became stronger in our commitment to serving others, more able in that effort, and filled with gratitude, as this Associate describes:

> Looking back on the past few months, I have noticed that service towards humanity has become a part of my life. I have gained a sense of peace within myself as a result of sacrificing a bit of myself for helping others. I am able to say what is important to me in life and also to appreciate what it has to offer me. Serving and trusting God takes faith and my faith has grown tremendously due to my work at [my placement] and community living.[130]

While our small communities were the most critical site for formation, our sense of community as Associates did not end there. Our common experiences as Associates moved us beyond our small communities to a sense of identity and belonging with other Holy Cross Associates. One Associate writes with surprise at this realization.

I didn't think I had that much in common with anyone outside my house and it never occurred to me that we all would be sharing

---

130 David Quinn, "From Massachusetts," *Holy Cross Associates Newsletter* (January 1996), USPAC.

similar experiences in the next year. The retreat in Portland reminded me how wrong I was. There was a bond forming between all of us this entire year and it was the time spent in Portland together that exemplified this connection . . . The most interesting part is that the whole relationship was forming without the least inclination to me. It's hard to imagine how it happens. How is it that forty people doing such different ministries can be brought together so closely, without ever realizing it? Simple. God.[131]

Certainly, organizers of the program fostered this sense through communication and events, including midyear retreats that brought all the US houses together and US Associate Thanksgiving gatherings in Hayward in the program's early years, as well as Christmases shared between members of nearby houses as the program grew, for those who could not go home. All of these were fitting activities and additional experiences of the formation characterized by and arising out of the Holy Cross family.

GENERATIONAL CHANGES AND THINGS THAT LAST

As I perused newsletters drawn from each period of the twenty-eight years of the Holy Cross Associates program, I found a remarkable consistency in most facets of Associates' experiences throughout the years and reflected in the stories told here. However, I did notice a few changes in Associate experiences and orientations with the different generations of Associates. They are worth mentioning here because they reflect generally the adaptability, learning, and growth achieved in the Holy Cross Associates as new cohorts coming into the program responded to changes in American society and the Catholic Church from the late 1970s to the early 2000s.

---

131 Julie Mayglothing, "From Massachusetts," *Holy Cross Associates Newsletter* (June 1996), USPAC.

There are two related shifts in how Associates talked about the pillars of the program as it moved from its first decade of existence into its second and third decades. First, the pillar of service, which was often twinned in the early years of the program with the concept of "ministry," gradually comes to be called service exclusively. After the first ten or fifteen years of the program, the term "ministry" almost never appears. While this could be read in different ways, I think this reflects an impulse to inclusivity among directors and Associates themselves with the advent of Generation X and the Millennial generation of Catholics. These generations tend to be less connected to institutions in general and churches in particular—making the language of ministry, with its rather direct connection to institutionalized church leadership, less fitting for some who might be questioning this connection while still attracted through their faith to service. Similarly, the pillar of prayer becomes twinned in later years with "spirituality," acknowledging that for Millennials, some of the traditional aspects of faith have become obstacles. With the conscious addition of spirituality, more of those attracted to the program could find their own faith lives more adequately reflected in the acknowledgment of the importance of an individual's interior spiritual life or even as a translation of what it means to pray. These shifts show HCA directors' responsiveness to the changing emerging adult demographic, in recognizing small but significant differences in how young people were being religiously shaped in a changing country and a changing church.

Perhaps counterintuitive, another trend in Associates' writings in the newsletters over time that is less reassuring is the absence of reflections of struggle over questions of women's leadership in the Catholic Church after the first ten or fifteen years of the program's existence. The HCA program was founded in an era of expectation and hope among many for the full inclusion of women into the church's leadership, including the possibility of ordaining women. In the Holy Cross Associates, women often found themselves in leadership roles, teaching, preaching, and leading prayer. We were encouraged by directors and formators to do so. Experiencing these possibilities for leadership but viewing a church where they were largely absent, some in the first generation of Associates wrote about painful struggles with the church and their desire to have women be in leadership roles not available to them. But gradually, these reflections diminished and disappeared from newsletters. One might think that it was a good thing that Associates were no longer voicing pain about issues of women in the church. However, this is not good news for American Catholicism, since it is most likely evidence of many Catholic women's growing sense of marginalization from institutional Catholicism and a reflection of numbers of formerly highly committed Catholic women who are leaving the church—a trend that has been documented in survey research over the past twenty-five years.[132]

There is one more generational change in the HCA program worth mentioning, and this is better news. Simply put, over the program's history, and especially in the first decade of its existence, Holy Cross religious and their lay partners gradually became more confident and assured of what each group had to offer. This led to a sharpening of orientation techniques and a growing integration of the work and presence of lay professionals as support for Associates, on the one hand, and a clarification and strengthening of the role of Holy Cross religious in formation, on the other.

As the program matured, Holy Cross priests and brothers grew in understanding that their primary gift to the Associates was found in their very tradition and experience of religious vocation. Orientation materials reflect in small ways—such as a schedule where a 10:00 p.m. "curfew" becomes the "Grand Silence" five years later. The congregation's expertise in formation, honed in the traditions

---

132 See, e.g., William V. D'Antonio, Michele Dillon, and Mary L. Gautier, *American Catholics in Transition* (Lanham: Rowman and Littlefield, 2003), and earlier books by William V. D'Antonio and his colleagues, including *American Catholics: Gender, Generation, and Commitment* (Walnut Creek, CA: Altamira Press, 2001).

and renewal of religious life, was recognized as a valuable gift to its lay Associates. After ten years, directors are able to report:

> [The Congregation of Holy Cross] has continued to be faithful to understanding lay ministry and assisting young men and women to understand themselves as church in the world . . . The Province has engaged itself in this formation. There are members of the Province who see it as integral to the mission of the Congregation and essential; who consider it primary in their responsibility of priesthood . . . While the program was earlier described as one of "collaborative ministry" . . . the collaboration is more clearly in the association which takes place between Holy Cross and these young men and women in the act of "forming."[133]

Indeed, this formation has had substantial, lasting, and even life-changing effects in the lives of Holy Cross Associates. Although I found no exhaustive roster of former Associates, I know through networks of former Associates that many have made lives of service to the poor and marginalized, in social service organizations as well as in the church. Many have pursued helping professions. Some have formed new intentional communities together, fashioned in various ways, often with other Associates and inclusive of spouses and children. Faith and spirituality remain important aspects of life for the many Associates with whom I am acquainted personally, no matter where their professional lives have taken them.

An Associate who participated during the program's inaugural years explains how many of the lasting effects of the program result from the formation that occurred in its intentional communities:

---

133 Jane Pitz, "Recommendations and Proposals: Holy Cross Associates Program" (1988), USPAC.

Community survival skills have developed into
interpersonal skills today. It was necessary for me to
open my mind to others' ideas, behaviors, and attitudes.
I learned to look beyond the surface for underlying
reasons. People have different backgrounds, motives,
and starting points that must be respected. On the
other hand, in order not to lose my identity, I learned
assertiveness and confrontation. Instead of sweeping
things under the rug, I had to openly deal with them. It
was there that I could be re-energized and centered . . .
I found strength in vulnerability. By giving power away
I became powerful. By seeing others through different
eyes, I achieved effective community living.

These experiences directly affected my choice of
vocation. I have spent the last four months in training
to be a sales engineer, but I do not consider this to
be my vocation. I define vocation in a much broader
context . . . My calling is the way I live. It is my
everyday attitudes, motivations, actions. And this is my
ministry today, to live out what I have learned, I am
learning about life and people.[134]

More generally, the lasting effects of the Associate year are perhaps
most obvious in the thorough integration of the values of simplicity,
community, faith, and service in the everyday lives and habits of
former Associates. Sometimes this appears in ordinary, almost
imperceptible ways. The HCA newsletter documenting the Associates'
twenty-fifth anniversary reveals this briefly and straightforwardly.
A report of discussions at the Brockton house celebration says

---

134 "How Does a Volunteer Program Change One's Life?" Report on the Holy Cross Associates
   program (1990), USPAC.

simply, "The most common theme that was shared [during mass and discussions afterward] was a feeling that the Associate program had made a positive impact on how each person continued to lead their lives—both as single individuals and as married couples with families—long after they participated in the program."[135] And in Chicago, a Mass and picnic included several families with children, who "enjoyed hot dogs and burgers with a delicious assortment of 'potluck' sides. It was a perfect setting to catch up with old friends and to meet new ones. I can't report that we hit on any profound insights that day but, in a small way, we did something good. In HCA style, we gathered a bunch of really great people together around tables for some prayer, conversation, and fun."[136]

A reflection from a former Associate written just a few years earlier elaborates on these sentiments and the questions we still reflect upon. She recalls "the life-transforming impact [the Associates] had for me, as well as the inspiration and challenge provided by these people and experiences."[137] The questions we struggled with during our HCA year were now integrated into her family's everyday life.

What does it mean to commit to Christian community in our home, neighborhood, world? In what ways are we and are we not living simply and what effect does that have? What part do we play in the injustices we see around us and how can we work toward social justice? In our daily lives are we living the things we say we believe?[138]

I venture to say that most of us also still live with our HCA memories and continue to live with—and ponder—these questions too.

---

135 Megan Dalsaso, "Celebration in Brockton," *The Anchor,* vol. III, no. 2 (Fall 2003), USPAC.
136 Rich Goode, "Holy Cross Associates Chicago Picnic, 2003," *The Anchor,* vol. III, no. 2 (Fall 2003), USPAC.
137 Karen Langlois Mertens, "New Staff!" *The Anchor,* vol. I, no. 1 (Winter 1999–2000), USPAC.
138 Ibid.

CHAPTER 8

Learning to Fail: Lay Formation and the Holy Cross Associates

Bill Cavanaugh

When I signed up to go to Chile with the Holy Cross Associates in 1987, a friend and former Holy Cross seminarian told me, "Good luck. I'm sure you'll do fine, though it would probably be better for you if you failed." I recall thinking, "Thanks a lot. It would probably be better for you if you got hit by a bus." But at some level I knew he was right.

I had already completed one tour of duty as a Holy Cross Associate in Colorado Springs, followed by a master's degree in theology at Cambridge. I went to Chile in search of the vibrant church I had read and fantasized about, but I also went to Chile in an attempt to find or reinvent myself, to be converted to the person I wanted to be and was convinced I was not. Lay formation is about service to church and world, but it is inevitably personal; the search for God is also the search for self. Lay formation—in my case, anyway—was not so much a process of building up as it was of tearing down or opening up, so that I could receive the gifts of others.

I will explore some theological themes central to lay formation programs—the option for the poor, the universality of the church, and the vocation of the laity—as these relate to my own experience as a Holy Cross Associate in Chile. Other people's experience will be different, but I hope there is something here that will resonate with you.

OPTION FOR THE POOR

"Today I've got diarrhea, a zit in my ear, and fleas." Thus begins my journal entry from January 29, 1988. There is a certain amount of bravado in the entry, but the romantic view of poverty tends to evaporate when little creatures are sucking your blood. Poverty is not true poverty if it is temporary, but nevertheless there was something formative about the sheer physicality of being there in a poor neighborhood in Santiago under the military dictatorship. Poverty is not just a theological theme when you are taking an ice-cold shower or being robbed at gunpoint. The not-temporary sufferings of our neighbors were, of course, much more profound: the small shacks with tarpaper roofs, the arbitrary arrests and torture, the times when there was literally no food in the house. As Associates we witnessed the suffering up close; privacy is in short supply in the *población*, and we were constantly in people's houses and lives and they in ours. Though we worried about being mere tourists of poverty, there was something about simply physically *being there* that was indelible. Our lives in the United States were carefully constructed with walls to prevent seeing what we could not help but see in Santiago: the real world, what I described in my journal as "long sleepless nights of a billion tears, people covering the planet for whom the sun never rises."

I wish I could claim that my journal is filled with such attempts at eloquence, but reading through it now after a quarter century has been a penitential practice of recalling how clueless I was. Many of my entries are self-absorbed musings filled with loneliness and insecurity, rehashing little tiffs and intra-house intrigues with my community members, or trying to figure out exactly what use I was to the people I supposedly came to serve. In my twenty-some years on the planet I had learned to read books and take exams, but I had not learned properly how to drive a nail, something that would have come in handy on the construction project I was allegedly helping to coordinate. I had learned Spanish in school, but it had done little to prepare me for the sounds with which my neighbors cheerfully assaulted me. My cluelessness could get me both in and out of trouble. When the neighborhood drug addicts I had befriended took me across the street for a beer, I discovered too late that we were in a house of prostitution. I extricated myself by talking about working for the church, upon which the owner, pistol in belt, asked whether I could put in a word for him with the priests, since he wanted to get married at the chapel.

My housemates and I swapped such stories on a regular basis, and such situations came to seem normal after a while. The HCA experience in Chile was a couple of years of high drama, punctuated by street protests and the plebiscite, a vote of yes or no on eight more years of General Pinochet. There were times when I felt overwhelmed by too much reality. The experience was exhilarating and disorienting. The disorientation, I gradually came to see, was crucial to the process of formation. What it meant to share the lot of poor people for a couple of years was not so much about drinking powdered milk and getting fleas as it was about sharing a deeper sense of powerlessness. Being not-poor means being able to draw on a lifetime of education and other interior resources that create the illusion that life can be managed and controlled. To be disoriented, on the other hand, is to be out of control. I found that I could not rely on my own resources and talents, as I was accustomed to doing, and had to rely on other people, housemates and Chilean friends, and ultimately on God. I had never searched for God with such urgency as I did during my years in Chile. A theological education sometimes gives the false impression that

God can be managed. The HCA experience for me was a thorough education in the fatuity of that impression.

I suppose that something like this was what my friend was trying to get at when he told me it would be good for me to fail. Powerlessness is ultimately what is true about human life. I don't think that poverty automatically produces reliance on God—in some it produces reliance on alcohol, etc.—but there was no missing the depth of the Good Friday Stations of the Cross procession that wound its way through the streets of Peñalolén. Karl Marx thought that such religion was opium for the poor, but I have been convinced that nearly the exact opposite is the case: wealth and privilege are a drug that deludes people into thinking that they do not need to rely on God.

One of the fruits of reliance on others is forgetting the self. One of my journal entries reads, "I'm beginning to turn outward and not look at myself constantly," an optimistic assessment that seems not to apply to the very next entry. At a certain stage, the spiritual life encourages navel gazing, constant self-examination and self-critique, usually by way of comparison with others. Living in community can encourage a sort of competition for who can have the deepest spiritual insight, work the hardest, or have the poorest friends. At its best, however, community encourages laughter, including and especially laughing at oneself. My HCA housemates and I did our share of crying, but we also laughed a lot and threw parties and did silly unprintable things. We were pretty good at breaking each other out of our solemnity and self-absorption. As the spiritual life progresses, self-forgetting becomes much more important than self-examination. At some point, the sensible soul simply gives up trying to micromanage the spiritual life and to make oneself better. The process is aided by other people breaking down barriers, barging into our house as Chileans are wont to do, or, in one case, hiding our coats so we couldn't leave a party, despite the fact that it was 2:00 a.m. Little kids were especially good at breaking down barriers, coming up in the street and taking me by the hand and leading me where they wanted me to go. The hand of God is surely in this. Vocation is being called out of one's self and into a wider life with God and other people.

Option for the poor is an experience of vulnerability that makes the exchange of gifts possible. I received so many gifts: Margarita fed me bowls of *cazuela* (Chilean soup) when I didn't want to eat my own cooking; Luchín made me laugh and made me stop being busy all the time; Rosa seemed to know when I needed an *abrazo* (hug); Hugo insisted that building projects are impossible without parties; Blanca always had caramels in her pocket. I gave gifts too—my time, my presence, my organizational skills, my humor—but once the barriers came down, it is probably more accurate to say that gifts weren't so much given from one person to another but just happened in the space opened up by the grace of God. As I wrote in my journal on what was not really a very good day, "To rejoice and give thanks I think is the most important thing on Earth."

THE UNIVERSALITY OF THE CHURCH

One day I was having tea in our house with our neighbor Blanca when my housemate Margy brought home three of her confirmation students from St. George's, the Holy Cross school on the other side of town. Blanca concluded the introductions by saying to the students, hospitably and sincerely, "Welcome to Chile."

The students were Chileans, born and raised in Santiago. They were tall, with light skin and hair and with nice teeth and clothes. Blanca was also Chilean, but four-foot-something, with dark skin and hair and just a few visible teeth. She could be excused for mistaking the students for foreigners. They lived in a different country, in a very real sense. Chile, like much of the world, was and remains sharply divided between rich and poor.

As Associates, we were remarkably well received by our neighbors, although they knew that we came from the United States. We were the Coneheads on the block, accepted for trying to blend in despite our funny accents and other peculiarities. A pair of St. George's graduates studying law who moved into our neighborhood as part of their Christian option for the poor, however, told us that it was more difficult for them than for us. They were the all-too-familiar enemy in a divided and conquered country.

One of the most valuable aspects of my time in Chile was experiencing the catholicity of the Catholic Church, the way that the Body of Christ transcends national boundaries. Experiencing the diversity of Catholicism was invigorating for someone bored of the suburban American version. On a trip during language school in Cuernavaca to a town called Santiago in Mexico, I scribbled in my journal, "I am of a completely different religion than that of the Catholics of Santiago, Mexico." Fortunately, that was hyperbole, not truth. In Santiago, Chile, I discovered by going to Mass and participating in a base community that Catholicism gave my Chilean friends and me a common culture and a common bond. My housemates and I were instantly accepted as sisters and brothers in Christ. It was reassuring to know that, hanging upside down on the bottom of the Earth, I still knew what I was doing at Mass. At the same time, we were able to see and participate in an active Catholicism unique to the circumstances of Pinochet's Chile.

Crossing national borders is, in some ways, the easy part. What is more difficult is crossing the class divide. The universal church includes both rich and poor and offers the hope that the borders between classes can be transgressed. In practice, it is hard. The Holy Cross Associates generally took graduates of privileged universities such as Notre Dame and sent them to work with poor people. Even if such graduates were not originally from privileged backgrounds, Notre Dame is itself a formation in the idea that graduates are meant to achieve power in order to make a positive difference in the world. Universities often encourage students to become universal subjects, viewing the world from above, as it were. Such an education makes one a foreigner in any poor community, at home or abroad.

A few weeks after arriving in Chile, my housemates and I were guests at Thanksgiving dinner at the American ambassador's house, thanks to a connection made by a Holy Cross priest. If my journal is accurate, I made a pig of myself, in the knowledge that my next turkey and pumpkin pie were likely several years away. Upon returning to Peñalolén, my housemates and I stepped off the bus into an angry crowd in front of the church. As ransom for a kidnapped colonel, an armed group had arranged for food to be distributed via certain select parishes in poor neighborhoods. Arrangements had been made for an orderly distribution, but when the food truck arrived, people began grabbing what they could get their hands on, leaving others with nothing. Those who were supposed to receive food but didn't were now milling about in front of San Roque in a foul mood. My belly was full. More significantly, I had *access*; I was only one degree of separation from the American ambassador.

The solution to the class divide is usually thought to be this: use your access to help the poor. Places such as Notre Dame marinate students in the rhetoric of going forth to change the world. I worry, however, that the world has had quite enough of well-meaning Americans trying to change it, as the history of Chile can attest. The history of "development" is a history of coercion from start to finish. Grand schemes to change the world from above too often result in more disempowerment for those whose world is being upended.

When my time as an Associate was finished, I came back to the United States because I had no marketable skills to offer Chile. Without Holy Cross support, I was unemployable. I was also ready to come home; I am a middle-class American. I worked for a while at the Notre Dame Law School on a database for human rights abuses, using the microfilmed archives of Archdiocese of Santiago's Vicariate of Solidarity. Then I went to Duke, where my doctoral dissertation drew on my time in Chile and my work on the archives of the Vicaria to examine the church's response to human rights abuses under the Pinochet regime. I returned to Chile for a few months to conduct interviews and gather materials. The project turned into my first book, entitled *Torture and Eucharist: Theology, Politics, and the Body of Christ.* I examined the use of torture and disappearances as a way of atomizing and disappearing social bodies between the state and the individual. I then looked at church practices, based in a theology of the Eucharist, that helped to reknit social bodies and make the Catholic Church the biggest thorn in Pinochet's side. Throughout the book, my emphasis is on grassroots organizations of Chileans. Much of my subsequent academic career in Christian social ethics has been taken up with critiques of the state and an emphasis on what is sometimes called micro-politics, the efforts of people to organize themselves and create alternative social spaces that escape the domination of states and transnational corporations.

My experience in Chile has helped convince me that our approach to bridging the class divide should be based not so much on gaining access to power as on empowering poor people to make a life for themselves. Our point of view should not be from above but from below. How to tell the difference is not always clear, and I certainly don't speak on these matters from a place of unambiguous purity. I write from a comfortable perch in academia. If becoming a universal subject is illusory, then I have to acknowledge my own inability to shed my middle-class identity.

VOCATION OF THE LAITY

The Holy Cross Associates program was part of a movement among religious orders to implement the Vatican II call to recognize the vocation of the laity in the church. The role of laypeople before the Second Vatican Council was stereotypically to "pray, pay, and obey," as the old saying went. There was a two-tiered ethic in which the counsels of perfection were for the clergy and vowed religious, while the laity were held to a lower standard and not expected to lead in the church. Vatican II changed course and called the laity to holiness, even to "perfection," as *Gaudium et Spes* put it. Lay associate programs were started as a way to allow laypeople to participate in that call; they were also a response to the recognition by religious orders that in the post–Vatican II world there might be fewer nuns, brothers, and priests to handle all the work that needed to be done. Laypeople would help in the work of the order.

One of the challenges programs such as the Holy Cross Associates faced was that the laypeople who signed up were mostly fresh out of college and, like me, underformed in the Christian life. We had had some theology classes and had attended our share of Masses, but for the most part our participation in the church had been passive. We did not know how to pray in a disciplined way, we did not really know how living in community was meant to be different than having housemates, our sense of the church's tradition was piecemeal at best, and we had little experience of lay leadership in the church. Our rawness made us susceptible to a shallow radicalism, what one Holy Cross priest in Chile mordantly called the "Patty Hearst syndrome." Inexperience in the Christian life was compounded by the fact that most of us had no skills that were applicable to our job placements. When I became a full-time high school teacher in my first tour of duty with HCA in Colorado Springs, I was twenty-one and had no experience teaching whatsoever. I arrived at the high school two weeks before the start of classes, the head of the religion section gave me some of the books I would be using ("I'll see if I can find that other teacher's manual around here somewhere"), and he told me "Good luck." I needed it.

The fact is that religious orders in the first couple of decades after Vatican II were just as inexperienced at running lay associate programs as the laypeople were at being associates of a religious order. It was on-the-job training for all involved. A couple of Irish laywomen my housemates and I met in language school in Cuernavaca had signed up with a religious order's lay associate program to help out at a school in an indigenous community in Mexico; they got to the village and were told that they *were* the school. Another young married couple I knew, recently graduated from college, signed up with a religious order to work at an orphanage in Bolivia; upon arrival, they were given the keys and put in charge of the entire operation. Some religious orders, strapped for priests and religious, saw lay volunteers as an answer to personnel shortages. This was not my experience with Holy Cross. Formation for us laypeople was, however, fairly informal. Our director, a Holy Cross priest or brother, would have dinner with us once a week. There was little in the way of a program of formation. We were not, for example, taught how to pray; our communal experiences of prayer consisted largely of staring at a candle and trying not to fall asleep.

Having said that, the informal process of formation was very formative; being around Holy Cross brothers, priests, nuns, and seminarians gave me a sense for living a Christian life that I could have gotten in no other way. As Associates, we were included in Holy Cross gatherings, parties, masses, retreats, and meetings. We worked side by side with vowed members of the community. I went on a preaching mission to a rural area with a group of seminarians. Members of Holy Cross were—all of them—kind and generous with us, and some went out of their way to befriend us. I was marked by my interactions with Holy Cross. Fr. Jim Schultz brought alive the concept of the wounded healer to me and gave me a glimpse of a prayer life of deep and tender intimacy with God. Fr. Tom McNally was a model of kindness and humility, a man who radiated a sense of goodness and joy that no language barrier could prevent people from seeing. Br. Bob Dailey was a crucial support for me at a time when I felt overwhelmed; he conveyed to me a sense of Christ as brother and friend that I have never forgotten.

I could go on in this vein and name many more vowed members of Holy Cross who formed me deeply. But what is important to note is not simply that there were and are a lot of great people in Holy Cross; there are a lot of great laypeople too who have formed me. What is important is that there is something about vowed religious life that made these people who they were; a structured prayer life and disciplines for discernment come immediately to mind. There is something that being around vowed religious has contributed to my formation that I would have been much less likely to have picked up by hanging around with laypeople, even in an intentional community. One of those things, I think, is that permanent vows make the intention in community less important. Once vows are made— intentionally, of course—there is a sense that the vowed person no longer chooses with whom to make community. These are the people God has stuck me with, and I am called to make a life with them. As a wise Holy Cross priest once said, "Ninety percent of the religious life is just showing up." Holy Cross was made of ordinary people, many with quirks, as their community members were sometimes keen to point out over a beer. But it was deeply formative to see such people commit for life to loving God in the company of others similarly committed to God and to each other. In a transient society that prizes freedom from others—keeping our options open—above all else, vowed religious life is a deeply countercultural witness. It is a way of loving God and loving neighbors with a deep sign value for the lay apostolate. We are all called to love those whom we do not choose.

We are all called to remain faithful to God and to others, even when we don't feel like it.

I have been talking about lay formation primarily because I am writing this piece from my own experience, but I think it is also the case that people in religious life are formed by their experience with laypeople. My evidence here is purely anecdotal, but people in religious life are happier when they have sustained contact with laypeople. Holy Cross religious sought us out because they liked to be around laypeople, especially women. As Pope Francis has intuited, healthy religious life is sustainable by immersion in the world, not by viewing the world as an occasion of sin. The priesthood today is unhealthy and unsustainable if it is seen as an elite corps of men who need to be kept unsullied. To allow religious to be formed by sustained contact as equals with laypeople entails risks; the cases of former Holy Cross seminarians marrying former Holy Cross Associates caused heartburn for some in the order. But I think that most recognized at some level that one of the vocations of the laity is to help form the clergy.

The Holy Cross Associate program was shut down in 2007; the official reasons given in the announcement were "loss of focus" in the program itself and waning interest in the program among both laypeople and Holy Cross religious. The order pledged to find new and more fruitful ways to collaborate with laypeople. From the point of view of a layperson, there are certainly plenty of other avenues for lay ministry in the church. In some ways, the lay apostolate has come of age in the decades since Vatican II. It is now not so rare to see laypeople in leadership positions in Catholic parishes, universities, and other organizations. There is no end in sight to the shortage of priests and religious, so it is imperative that laypeople take the lead and find ways of lay-led formation. It must be acknowledged, however, that the average layperson today is not well formed; I have seen the average literacy in the faith among my nominally Catholic students shrink in my twenty years of teaching undergraduates. Collaboration between laypeople and religious orders is not the only remedy, but it is one that I hope is not overlooked. The gap between clergy and religious on the one side and laity on the other is one that Vatican II has challenged us to close, and Pope Francis has renewed that call in many ways, including his criticisms of clericalism. I would hope that laypeople and religious do not choose to go their separate ways but find ways to contribute to each other's formation.

One of the last journal entries I wrote before leaving Chile reads, "Before it's too late, I must realize that life is not for helping or achieving; it is for living." I know what Teresa of Avila meant when she said that "God has no hands but yours," but God does not need us. The point of a lay volunteer experience is not to rescue God from helplessness. God changes the world, not us. By our own efforts, we fail, but God makes a way for us. In the most real sense, we do not form each other; we are formed by God in the space of hospitality that God opens up among us.

CHAPTER 9

From Notre Dame to Chile and Back:
Living Faith and Justice

Lou Nanni

After graduating from the University of Notre Dame in 1984, I set out to live and work among the poor for two plus years in the Santiago, Chile, shantytown of Penálonén. I was part of the Holy Cross Associates program, a lay missionary effort with placements in both the United States and abroad. By any standard, I could not have been better prepared for this twenty-eight-month, cross-cultural, overseas service engagement.

Father Don McNeill, C.S.C., and his crack team at the newly formed Center for Social Concerns had given us many opportunities to immerse ourselves in service while students at Notre Dame. During my first year, I participated in the Urban Plunge, a forty-eight-hour immersion into the seediest and most blighted areas of Buffalo, New York, the nearest city to where I grew up. In Fr. Don fashion, we read articles and discussed the dynamics of urban poverty prior to our excursion. After forty-eight hours of sensory overload, we took a course reflecting on our Christian call to respond to the needs of those marginalized all around us.

The Urban Plunge prompted me to become a Big Brother in the local chapter of the Big Brother–Big Sister program over the next three years. An eight-year-old African American boy nicknamed Puggy became a core part of my Notre Dame education and, more poignantly, family. Through Puggy and the plight of his siblings and alcoholic mother, I found myself grappling each week with Gospel-level questions. How am I to discipline this young boy without having him believe that my love is conditional or that I too might walk out on him? Where do my Christian responsibilities begin and end, given the depth and diversity of needs in this one little boy? These and many similar experiences through the Center for Social Concerns led me to heed the call to a deeper level of Christian service in Santiago.

I departed Notre Dame as a confident and curious young man. I was wide-eyed, naive, and ready for a challenge, or so I thought. Mark Twain once commented, "If you have confidence and ignorance, success is virtually assured." I felt good about myself, my circle of friends, my hunger to learn and grow, and, ultimately, my commitment to be of service to others in need. In less than one year, my self-esteem had deteriorated, and I was consumed with despair. I couldn't believe how far down the ladder I traveled in such a short time. I was overcome by hungry faces of little children everywhere in our shantytown; by teenagers who would valiantly lie to themselves about options that didn't exist and dreams never to be fulfilled; by fathers whose inert bodies littered dirt roads as they lay facedown drunk to escape the shame, at least momentarily, of not being able to feed and clothe their children. And yet what disgusted me most was the discovery that their lives far more closely reflected the living conditions of the world's majority than did mine. I was haunted to learn how much my wealth set me apart.

Of course, I arrived in Chile wide-eyed with hope and enthusiasm. I knew the challenges before me were formidable, but I was convinced that I could make an impact, even if it were modest. I began by standing before forty-one sixth-graders the first day of class. I had envisioned their angelic faces awaiting my care and guidance. Every Thursday from 4:30 to 6:00 p.m. I was charged with teaching them English. Andacollo was a hybrid school run by the Catholic priests of the Congregation of Holy Cross, with supplemental funding from the government. The old adobe brick buildings were located south of downtown and catered primarily to children from a violent and destitute shantytown on the outskirts of Santiago called Pudahuel. The dirt paths that led from one classroom to the next were well worn. Dust filled the warm air as high school students used the buildings in the morning, after which elementary students filled the same classrooms from afternoon until early evening.

I had received no training as a teacher and was completely new to the culture and language. I looked anything but the part of a teacher. I was a scrawny one hundred forty-five pounds, having lost eighteen pounds since my arrival due to a bad case of parasites and amoebas. My head looked oversized with big curly brown hair, and my jeans were perpetually so dirty (I was a bit slack as we washed our clothes by hand) that a fellow teacher commented that they'd be too slippery for a cat to latch onto. I also looked like I was sixteen years old, frequently mistaken as a high school student. If this weren't enough, I was asked to teach a foreign language to children who would struggle most of their lives to read and write their own language. Nevertheless, I thought, If only I could love them and show them a positive example, who knows how much good that might do? It was clear just ten minutes into the first day of class that I was not ready for the challenge before me. Like a weak swimmer in turbulent waters, I spent every ounce of energy just trying to keep afloat. The classroom was mass pandemonium, and, despite my best efforts, my weak Spanish incited laughter and convinced the students that they were running the show, which wasn't far from the truth.

In the front of the classroom sat Manuel. He was an unruly boy, standing out even among his restless peers. It didn't take long to figure out that he was the bully of the classroom. The other students held him in fear and respect. He was clearly the leader. Amid all the chaos—in a classroom barely illuminated by a naked light bulb that dangled from the ceiling by a single wire and where students sat two to a desk built for one—Manuel quickly began to get my attention and, for that matter, the attention of his classmates. He kept reaching over to touch the hair and shoulders of Liliana, who sat next to him, and then, looking me in the eyes, he repeated several times, "*Esta es mi polola*" ("This is my girlfriend"). It was immediately apparent that Liliana did not share his sentiments.

Three times I asked Manuel to take his hands off Liliana, and each time he ignored me. Finally, at a loss for what to do, I reverted to that ancient practice of putting him and his desk in the corner. Much to my surprise, it seemed to work. After a half hour or so, I spoke to him with all the positive reinforcement that I imagined a good teacher would use in such a situation. I told him that he had behaved very well and I was going to return him to his original place. Thinking the worst was over, I turned to write on the chalkboard when I heard Liliana's anguished cries and found Manuel groping her small breasts. The classroom for the first time fell silent, and I could feel the students looking on with keen interest to see how their bully, Manuel, would unravel this foreign prey.

My first real test and all the wrong motives came to the surface. This was my classroom, and I was determined not to lose control to a group of sixth-graders or to a bully shamelessly molesting an innocent little girl on center stage. I stared Manuel in the eye and, before forty hushed onlookers, told him as decisively as I could in my broken Spanish to leave the classroom. He defiantly glared back at me and boldly yet calmly said "No!" I was taken aback by his response. I hadn't contemplated the possibility of a no and was unsure what my next move should be.

Then as parents often do in helpless situations, I issued the same command, only this time with a louder and deeper voice that I hoped would reverberate with authority. To no avail, he still said no. Finally, I approached Manuel to physically remove him from the classroom, yet he surprised me again by cowering before me and pleading with me not to strike him. I grabbed hold of his bicep and ushered him out of the room and into the hallway. There, out of sheer frustration, I firmly pushed him up against the wall and asked him what he was doing. And almost simultaneously, I asked myself the same question: What was I doing?

I had traveled more than five thousand miles to live among and serve the poor, to learn from them and in the process to grow stronger in my Christian faith. Here I was on my first day of class pushing a troubled sixth-grade student against a wall out of exasperation. After class that day I gathered some additional information on Manuel and that evening called my father on the phone in search of counsel. He had dedicated much of his life as both a teacher and an administrator in primary and secondary education. I explained the situation to him. The classroom was overcrowded with hungry and malnourished children. There was no lunch program, and most survived daily on a bowl of clear broth and a piece of bread. Each day an elderly woman would present herself to the class and choose five students from a list attached to a clipboard in her hands. All the students waved their arms excitedly in the air when she entered, and most fell back in their seats dejected when she left. The five children fortunate to be chosen that day were each granted a glass of milk. Apparently, there just wasn't enough to go around.

There were no textbooks. The students had one basic notebook for all classes for the entire year and usually one pen as well. As a teacher, your only tools were a piece of chalk, the board, and whatever creativity you could muster that day. There were no teacher conferences or faculty meetings to share information and coordinate curriculum. Teachers were paid so miserably that most taught in two or three different schools just to get by, with as many as seventy hours of class time each week. In the winter months of June through August, temperatures would hover in the thirties and forties. There was no heat in the classroom, and I taught in a wool hat, gloves, down vest, and coat before students who sat in front of me barely clad against the cold.

And then there was Manuel. I had learned that he was the thirteenth of fourteen children. He came from one of the toughest parts of one of the worst shantytowns. While he didn't have to be at school until 1:00 p.m., he awoke every day at 5:00 a.m. with two older brothers to search the streets for cardboard that could be turned in for loose change to buy bread for his family. Manuel was, in fact, violent. He looked gruff and strong, a miniature man squeezed into a tattered school uniform two sizes too small. His face was worn, and his dry, unruly hair was half-combed from left to right, as if in the wrong direction. All of the students at Andacollo and most of the teachers feared him. He had been kicked out of public schools the past two years for disciplinary reasons. This was his third and final shot at the sixth grade, thanks to this Catholic school that was not yet willing to give up on him. Not only did he suffer the constant pangs of hunger but also he was completely illiterate. Ironically, I was charged to teach him English. "Dad," I asked that night from an underground public telephone station located near the subway, "what should I do?"

After commiserating with me for a moment about the challenging classroom situation, he said there was only one thing I could do for Manuel. Try to become his best friend. Spend as much time with him outside the classroom as possible. Love him. And so I began with renewed vigor to get to know the real Manuel—the child hidden behind the tough exterior. I set out not only to become his friend but also to break down the watertight wall he had built around himself to keep all others out.

After every class Manuel and I would walk together the twenty blocks or so to catch a bus that would take him to his shantytown, then on to mine. This kept us from having to pay for two buses. Several months went by without any visible sign of progress. One day when we were walking, he said to me in the tone of a penitent confessing his sins: "Teacher"—he was fond of calling me "teacher" in English—"I sometimes beg for money on the streets. I know it's wrong, but I swear I give the money to my mother for food." I told him that I didn't see anything wrong with it, granting him the absolution he was seeking for this noble little sin. On another occasion during a walk together, he spied an abandoned cardboard box and then grasped for it as if he had stumbled upon a lost treasure. I tried to share his joy and, at the same time, conceal my horror.

Finally, at the end of our walk one evening, Manuel's wall came tumbling down. As a special treat, I invited him to join me for a bite at a restaurant—more like a drab, little deli with three small round tables and terribly thin wax-paper-like-napkins upon them. I could see that Manuel for some reason was ill at ease. I ordered two hot dogs and two Cokes, trying to keep it simple. Manuel was out of his element and looked unusually uncomfortable as he sat at the table. It is ironic, but of all things it was the hot dog that triggered his wall to come down. When it arrived at the table, Manuel glanced at me with this painful look in his eyes. He was ashamed. He didn't know how to eat the hot dog. I realized then that in his thirteen years he had never brought a morsel of meat to his mouth.

In that poignant moment when I looked into his big brown vulnerable eyes, I saw the wounded animal that was Manuel, hidden so well behind a thick wall. It was not pretty. Here was the child who society had said it doesn't matter that you're deprived of food and unable to concentrate on anything beyond your empty stomach. Here was the child who society had said it doesn't matter that you're defenseless against the elements living in a destitute one-room shanty, built with scraps in the same way a bird builds a nest. Here was the child who society had said that it doesn't matter when you're sick that you get medical attention. Here was the child who society had said that it doesn't matter if you ever learn to read and write or that your God-given talents go undeveloped in this world. In fact, Manuel, you don't matter. You are insignificant, unimportant, and not worthy of our attention.

Perhaps what was most disconcerting of all was my reaction. Over two hotdogs I sat horrified and said quietly to myself, "Manuel, put your wall back up; it hurts too much to see it down."

I fell hard during that first year in Chile. I lost faith in God, in humanity, and in myself. I lost my will to live. I asked myself every morning as I awoke for several months on end: Why go on? I had just turned twenty-three years old. I knew that Manuel was not alone; in fact, his story was repeated over and over in countless children throughout the world. I knew from data collected by Catholic Relief Services (the US Catholic Church's division for outreach to the world poor) that fifty percent of the world's population was either homeless or subjected to substandard housing conditions and was without adequate, safe drinking water. Forty-seven percent were illiterate. Thirty-five percent suffered from acute hunger and malnutrition. Six percent were US citizens and possessed thirty-three percent of the world's income while consuming forty percent of the planet's unrenewable resources. A staggering fifty-five percent had an annual income of less than six hundred US dollars. And finally, one percent of the world's population had a college education. No, Manuel was not alone in his misery . . . but I was in my privilege.

I was plagued with questions such as how twenty-four thousand persons could be permitted to die of malnutrition every day, mostly young children, in a world where the grain supply alone was enough to meet everybody's nutritional needs one and a half times over. In Peñalolén these questions ceased to be academic or philosophical. They were no longer numbers, statistics, or stories I read about. They now had names and faces, and they were my students, my neighbors, and my friends. Manuel seemed to embody, in one small child, all of the world's despair, and yet, paradoxically, he did not even begin to scratch its surface.

I could never have recognized it then, but during my first year in Chile I was blessed with the terrible gift that is despair. Most people in this world are broken down before age twenty-three. Some never are. It is a terrible thing to lose hope. I believe that it is the greatest of all suffering and the worst of all sin. It does, however, bring you into communion with so many other lost souls in this world. Renowned physician and peacemaker Dr. Albert Schweitzer spoke about a "fellowship of those who bear the mark of pain." When a person is contemplating suicide, if he or she seeks anyone's help, he or she will likely talk with somebody who at one point lost his or her will to live. The gift of healing is best given by the one who knows suffering. The catch is that when a person loses hope, he or she is convinced that he or she will never find it again.

I worked long days and cried myself to sleep many nights during my first year in that Santiago shantytown. Never before had I served so passionately and so completely, and never before had I felt so poorly about myself. I was haunted by the depth and diversity of need that surrounded me during every waking moment and equally tormented by my inability to be the selfless servant that I had hoped I would be. At some level, I despised the fact that my eyes had been opened and no longer could I hide comfortably behind the cloak of blindness and denial. Not only was there so much hunger and poverty but also there was wicked oppression against any caring soul who tried to confront the injustice. Instruments of the right-wing military dictatorship of General Augusto Pinochet tortured three of my high school students. Most were victims of the *picana* method, where they were blindfolded and stripped naked and then fastened to a bare set of metal-framed bunk beds. Jolts of electric current were applied to their genitalia, on and off for five days on end. I also visited twenty-five women political prisoners every Saturday morning, all of whom had suffered similar forms of torture. Only in their cases, most were gang-raped and a few left carrying in their wombs the children of their torturers.

I cried for Christ crucified in these anguished souls afflicted by poverty and oppression. Yet it was not the military regime or its instruments of death that troubled me most. My soul was plagued even more by the indifference of the masses. Why weren't more people outraged? Where were all the so-called religious persons of this world? I was haunted by the image of a young Jew, Elie Wiesel, who describes in his book *Night* how as a twelve-year-old boy he, his mother, father, and sister Tzipora were loaded like cattle and shipped in a train to a concentration camp. At Buchenwald, they saw the smokestacks and smelled the terrible stench of burnt flesh.

As they exited the train, Elie and his father, separated now from his mother and sister, began to walk in a long line headed directly for the smokestacks. As the fear grew, the roles reversed, and the twelve-year-old boy tried to comfort his father saying, "Do not worry, father, humanity will not let this happen to us." Distraught, his father responded, "Humanity, my son, doesn't give a damn." His father was right. Seven million Jews were murdered, thirteen million overall in German concentration camps. Elie's father, mother, and little sister, Tzipora, were among them. Some would argue that the indifference of the masses killed them even more than the Nazis.

During my first year in Chile, I was not unlike a person who just quit smoking and could not tolerate being around other smokers. Insecure in the commitment to stay smoke free, beginners are likely to lash out at those who threaten their newfound conviction. My eyes had been opened to a world full of despair, and I was indignant toward those who still couldn't or wouldn't see. My spirit was crushed. In the end, I discovered hope where I least expected to find it. I encountered persons whom I came to call "common-day prophets." These people were usually of modest means and gave of themselves in quiet yet heroic ways.

It was Magdalena, an eighth-grade student of mine who invited me to dinner at her family's very humble home. When bologna was served, I thought little of it until Diego, her little brother, unwittingly mentioned that this was the first time they had eaten meat in several years. I was humbled by a family who had every good reason to hoard the little they had and yet was able to give so purely, joyfully, and abundantly to make their gringo friend feel comfortable.

It was Lucho and Olga, our hard-working neighbors who together with their three young boys were barely getting by. On a cold, rainy day, I invited three high school seniors from a prestigious Santiago prep school to visit Peñalolén, for never in their lives had they been to a shantytown, even though destitution encircled their wealthy neighborhood. We stopped by Lucho and Olga's house. They served the customary tea with bread and jelly. Ten minutes into our visit, the paraffin fuel ran out of their little portable heater. Lucho discreetly slipped his oldest son, Pablo, a few pesos and sent him off to buy some more. Curious, I asked Pablo and he confirmed that they never used a heater in their home. They wanted their guests to feel comfortable— another quiet gift from the heart, full of sacrifice and joy.

Dona Elena was another common-day prophet. She was the single mother of four teenage children; her life never seemed to know a moment's rest. A pillar of strength for the neighborhood, she was a woman of faith who was committed first and foremost to her family but somehow seemed to have the time and compassion left over for everybody else who came to her door. When a teenager was tortured to death three neighborhoods over, Dona Elena was among the courageous few who protested his murder at a demonstration in the street. She knew full well that she risked orphaning her own children in the process. She didn't want to be out there protesting in the street, she explained, but her conscience would not permit her not to be there. Moreover, she added, the greatest gift she could pass on to her children was the concrete example of faith in God and love for others.

I think of the women political prisoners weekly as common-day prophets. Every Saturday morning I would take the subway walk to the San Miguel prison. Perhaps it was not so ironic that this prison was named after an angel and saint. At the gate I would present identification and recite my card number. This was how intelligence forces kept an eye on those who were visiting political prisoners. Then I would pass through a security check where we were frisked thoroughly. I would have many suspense-filled checks over the two years as I smuggled letters out for the women that were handwritten in letters smaller than the typed words on this page. I hid them in my underwear.

When I first met the women political prisoners, I was surprised to see that they did not fit my media-shaped image of revolutionaries or terrorists. Some looked like my mother. One was a physician, another a university professor, another an unemployed twenty-one-year-old from a shantytown. What they shared in common was an incredible empathy for the poor and oppressed people of their land. They not only heard the cry of the poor but also felt it. All were moved to the point of action, some violently and others nonviolently. All, without exception, suffered dearly for their convictions, as did their family members.

I remember early on trying to convince Miriam Ortega Araya, a petite, fiery middle-aged woman full of compassion and tenacity, that what Chile needed was a Martin Luther King Jr. or a Mahatma Gandhi to lead a nonviolent revolution with a soul-force based on love. She smiled and patiently explained how King and Gandhi could maneuver under the US and British systems of government but never would survive under a dictatorship such as Pinochet's. Here the trees of opposition were cut down before they could become anything more than saplings. Here leaders who threaten the status quo go to prison, never to be seen or heard from again. Miriam had been sentenced to death by the military tribunals for the attempted assassination of a military general who was appointed by the dictator as mayor of Santiago. She would neither deny nor confirm her involvement, but she argued that such a measure was justified given the atrocities perpetrated by this man and the regime.

Most of the political prisoners professed to be Marxist-Leninists, belonging to different factions of Communist parties. It is, of course, not uncommon to fight one extreme from the point of the other extreme. I came to love and respect these women regardless of what they called themselves. I wondered, if a Pinochet were ever to emerge in the States, who among my family and friends might find themselves imprisoned for their convictions like these women? In the end, even though few professed to be Christian, I found them to be more Christ-like than most people I know. They loved, risked, and suffered on behalf of others. And as far as I was concerned, the only Christians who could justly criticize their use of violence were the one percent who were already on the front line taking the same risks, only in a nonviolent manner.

I admired these women for their hospitality, their compassion, and their ability to hope even in the dark cells of torture and imprisonment. They welcomed me every Saturday morning with an affection and care that I have seldom experienced from anybody in any setting. When I left Chile, they gave me a gift that still sits on my desk to this day and helps me cherish the memory of these common-day prophets. It is a copper penholder engraved with the following verse:

You have come to know women
Who give off the fragrance of
Perfume and gun powder,
And whose wombs are as
Fertile as their consciences.

During my second year in Chile, I was moved to tears by Christ
resurrected in the people—persons able to testify to hope and
love even though their bodies suffered deprivation and violence.
These common-day prophets may have been few in number, but
the authenticity of their examples resuscitated in me a hope that I
thought I had lost forever. I knew that these few, marginal prophets
would leave a more indelible impression on my soul than the
thousands of people who led mainstream lives of indifference. No,
the answer would never be in numbers. Hope resides in the capacity
within each and every one of us to rise above our human frailties and,
even at great risk, to give joyfully and selflessly to others.

Manuel, by the way, dropped out of school that year. I never saw
or heard from him again.

What would happen spiritually to me if my family and all that
I possessed were stripped away, leaving me alone and on the streets?
The answer to this question was the cornerstone upon which I needed
to build my faith . . . a faith not dependent on things of this world.
I wished to find in the cracks of society—in abandoned buildings,
on street corners, under viaducts, and in shelters—living examples of
people who knew great despair but were not consumed by it. Were
there individuals among the homeless still courageous enough to
believe in a better future and work toward it? I knew that I would
be wading in treacherous waters on this journey, that ironically in
searching for hope I risked being consumed by despair.

I wanted to help build a community that transcended barriers
that typically separate us—socioeconomically, racially, culturally,

educationally, and along lines of ability. I knew that with creativity and compassion we could demonstrate that cycles of violence and despair can be broken. Social problems such as homelessness are formidable but not intractable. I was in search of common-day prophets among the homeless who, given the proper support, could lead us in building a new and better society. I was convinced that in their brokenness and marginalization the homeless were uniquely situated to unsettle and inspire us all to grow in our common humanity and to grow closer together as spiritual beings. In this land of wealth, I took to the streets in search of hope.

My experience in Chile led me to find hope where there is despair and to discover joy in places of sorrow. It takes faith, vision, and courage to not give up on our most vexing social problems such as hunger, homelessness, and indifference. We need to confront the cynicism that plagues our society today and not give up on ourselves or our capacity to make a difference. Change for the better is possible. The social problems of the day are not intractable. As Christians, we are called to dwell in the cracks of society and to embrace our own brokenness, for it is in weakness that we know the need for God and for others. Every crisis, personal or communal, brings with it an unprecedented opportunity for growth. We are called to resuscitate hope in the darkest recesses of our souls as well as in our communities. This is no small task, but what could possibly give us more joy and meaning than to tackle these challenges head-on?

I was blessed to return to Notre Dame after Chile, participating in the very first year of the master's program of the Kroc Institute for International Peace Studies. Once again, the Notre Dame family was there to guide me and help me to better understand my experiences in Chile. Mark Twain once quipped, "If a cat sits on a hot stove, it will never sit on a hot stove again; but, it will never sit on a cold one either." It was important for me to not extract too much from Chile and to put these experiences in the proper context. Following postgraduate study,

I worked for three years for the Catholic Diocese of Orlando, Florida, directing their sister diocese partnership in the Dominican Republic along the Haitian border. Once again, I was exposed to the paradox of destitution and joy.

I remember being confronted by the words of Mother Teresa while living among the poor in the Dominican Republic. She wrote that poverty in the United States is, in many ways, worse than in the Third World. Her point was twofold. First, poverty surrounded by wealth and excess leaves an individual to feel left out and insignificant. Second, she discovered in the United States a pervasive mentality in which the poverty of an individual is judged to be in direct proportion to a deficiency in character. People are perceived to be poor because of bad choices, because of a fault of their own. Mother Teresa explained that the greatest poverty in this world is not hunger for the physical—food, shelter, clothing—but rather a hunger for love and belonging.

In 1991, after five years of service in Latin America, I decided to work with persons who found themselves homeless in the United States. I wanted to reacquaint myself with despair yet this time in my own country. It is hypocritical to see poverty far away and yet never recognize it next door. It is also insulting. I wanted to compare and contrast poverty in the Third World—or what I prefer to call countries of underconsumption—with poverty in the United States, a country of overconsumption. I began working with the homeless because I needed to cross an invisible barrier in my own backyard. I was convinced that the only place I could find real hope was at the point of greatest despair.

I found myself called for the next eight years to work at the South Bend Center for the Homeless. I wanted to test Mother Teresa's theory. I was ashamed to know very little about poverty in my own backyard. I came to discover that the common denominator to homelessness is a pathology of connectedness. When a person hits the streets and reluctantly enters the doors of a shelter, it becomes a moment of abject recognition that all support systems have failed. The nurturing relationships, if they ever existed in the first place, can no longer be counted on. In fact, for many among the homeless, the term "rehabilitation" is a misnomer. One cannot be restored to a condition never experienced in the first place. Among the homeless, increasingly we find persons not who have fallen through the cracks of society but rather who are born in them. It is a tall order to transmit a new way of life to people who have known only brokenness, hardship, and self-sabotage. Let there be no misunderstanding: the challenge of transforming lives is daunting. There is no quick fix, no easy solution. But there are countless examples of miraculous transformations. The homeless population is filled with "common-day prophets" and inspiring stories of triumph and of hope among despair.

In 1999, I returned to the place that opened my eyes and set me on this path. For the past seventeen years I have been privileged to serve the Notre Dame mission as one among many administrators. My primary responsibilities involve oversight of our development operation and alumni association. It is a gift to work alongside colleagues and friends who regularly inspire me to not only do good work but also be a better person. Our mission is to fully develop the God-given potential of our students—intellectually, emotionally, physically, spiritually, and socially. Notre Dame, in the end, is about educating the next generation of leaders, with the goal every year to graduate students who will transform the jangling discord of this world into a more harmonic symphony. What could be more worthy of my modest efforts and limited abilities than to serve a university dedicated to the Mother of God and, inherent to the vision of its founder, Fr. Edward Sorin, to be one of the greatest forces for good in all of society?

CHAPTER 10

Canto Grande

Charles Kenney

*N*ot all architects design buildings. Some create spaces, networks, and relationships through which people encounter faith, hope, and love and from which they go out to share these with others, encountering, learning about, and transforming the world. Don McNeill is this kind of architect, building a church in collaboration with other men and women that seeks to respond to the needs of the world. Don McNeill has been the architect of much of my life, as he has shaped the lives of thousands of others.

I first encountered one of Don's life-changing spaces when I opened the *South Bend Tribune* one day and read about a local girl who had been detained by the military regime of General Augusto Pinochet in Chile. The girl was Kathy Osberger, my girlfriend, Peggy Osberger's older sister, and she was in Chile as a participant in one of the programs Don helped start, the Latin American Program of Experiential Learning (LAPEL). Months later, when Kathy came home after working in Chile and Peru, a conversation with her over the Christmas holiday sparked a decision that led me to Don McNeill in person.

In January 1977 I joined CILA (Council for the International Lay Apostolate), a student community mentored by Don and dedicated to the celebration of faith and service to others. CILA members engaged in service work during the school year, and some undertook intense summer service projects domestically and abroad. Don presided at the CILA Masses I attended and organized retreats, and through CILA I began my first service experience at the local Family and Children's Center. That I was not very good at what I did at the center mattered far less than the fact that I had gone out from the university and was encountering young men whose lives were lived in what seemed like a different universe than mine. The community Don helped build through CILA was both nurturing and challenging, and the amazing people I met in CILA enriched and inspired me in faith and action.

Also inspiring and challenging were former LAPEL participants such as Kathy Osberger and Bernie Nahlen, whose experiences in Chile and Peru led me to decide to apply to participate in the 1978–1979 LAPEL program. I worked with them and with a group of Chilean exiles at Notre Dame publishing information about Pinochet's human rights abuses in a newsletter sent around the country. LAPEL and CILA, two spaces of experiential learning formed by Don McNeill, had begun to change my life.

Although I had been with Don many times at CILA events, I was somewhat in awe of him as we sat down in Corby Hall in August 1977 to discuss my interest in the LAPEL program and the lengthy application process. As I had never studied Spanish, he suggested I begin at once, and he also suggested I enroll in a theology course he was teaching that fall, the Church and Social Action. I remember being deeply interested in questions of social justice, but the church writ large interested me hardly at all.

The Church and Social Action became the third community created by Don McNeill that shaped my life. Ours was a small class, and Don facilitated penetrating discussion and reflection in a way I had not yet experienced at the university. We read and debated key documents of the church's social teaching, from *Rerum Novarum* through the Second Vatican Council and into the 1970s, each of which was a revelation to me. The members of this small class shared their faith and their vision of a church I had never before imagined. I found language about "building the Kingdom" strange and challenging, and through this course I not only learned a great deal about social justice but also developed a deep interest in the church. I also read and wrote a research paper on Peruvian theologian Gustavo Gutiérrez's recently published *A Theology of Liberation* and its critics. I could not have imagined then that in a few years I would be working with Gustavo in Lima.

Over the Christmas break that year I participated in another of Don's life-changing experiential learning programs, the Urban Plunge. For two days and one night, a small group of Notre Dame and Saint Mary's students and I encountered the world of the inner-city poor in Gary, Indiana, a city then infamous as the murder capital of the United States. Our guide was a Chicago Catholic Theological Union professor who had been a missionary in South Africa and on American Indian reservations, Claude-Marie Barbour. At a distance of almost forty years, what I most remember is the dignity and respect she showed each of those from the community she had asked to meet with us to tell their stories: an unemployed young man on kidney dialysis; a working prostitute; an evangelical church pastor whom we first saw energetically leading his congregation in prayer and song in a red and black cape and with whom we then met later in his chambers to hear him explain in sophisticated terms his understanding of the role of his church in the life of the local community. We slept overnight in the basement of a house warmed by the kitchen oven and populated by young men going in and out and sleeping with no adult in sight. On Sunday, in addition to the evangelical church service, we attended a black Muslim mosque and Jesse Jackson's

Operation PUSH. For me, to discover these unknown worlds so very near the world in which I lived was astonishing; what I carried forth was a profound sense of the humanity and dignity of the persons we met. I had been to Appalachia and to the South Bronx, places of great and very different kinds of poverty, but this was the first time I experienced crossing over into another culture and encountering the persons there on their own terms.

Of all of the programs created by Don McNeill, none would shape my life more than the Latin American Program of Experiential Learning. LAPEL had as its avowed purpose the formation of competent and compassionate analysts and actors for justice in the world. By 1978 the program focused on intense insertion of students into the world of the poor in Lima, Peru. Over the length of a school year, we earned a semester of academic credit in five courses through instruction by Holy Cross priests in Lima and in correspondence and independent study with four Notre Dame professors: Ken Jameson (economics), Claude Pomerleau, C.S.C. (political science), Al LeMay (Spanish conversation and Peruvian literature), and Don McNeill (theology). We each chose research topics and wrote lengthy interdisciplinary theses in Spanish, incorporating what we learned experientially and through our academic research. We took these theses back with us to Notre Dame, where our professors read and commented on them and held oral exams with each of us, after which we were given grades.

Although I took intensive Spanish during one year at Notre Dame, audited a course on Quixote, and moved off campus to live with former LAPEL participants and a Holy Cross seminarian, my proficiency in Spanish was still low. For me, then, LAPEL began with a journey by van with Mexican migrants from Chicago to the border, a train to Mexico City, and language school in Cuernavaca, Mexico. Crossing the border at Laredo, I began my first encounter with the rich culture and deep history of Latin America.

My companion for the LAPEL year, the wonderful and indefatigable Fran Evans, joined me in Cuernavaca, and together we traveled by land through Central America and then by air to Ecuador and Peru. Our first stop was Mexico City, where we stayed with a friend in whose house we met two Peruvian journalists who had just been sent into exile by Peru's military government—a taste of what was to come. We traveled by bus through southern Mexico and Guatemala to El Salvador, where we were hosted by Maryknoll priests and sisters in the city of Santa Ana. This was shortly before full-scale civil war erupted, and tensions were already high, as the Maryknoll missionaries knew their work was becoming dangerous. (Over the next year, six priests would be murdered in El Salvador, and the following year saw the assassination of Archbishop Oscar Romero and the murder of four American churchwomen—lay missionary Jean Donovan, Ursuline Sister Dorothy Kazel, and two Maryknoll sisters, Ita Ford and Maura Clarke.) After a few days in El Salvador we continued through Honduras and Nicaragua, where the Sandinistas were fighting the Somoza regime; Costa Rica; and Panama, where we stayed with priests from the Diocese of Chicago in the poor neighborhood of San Miguelito.

When Fran and I arrived in Lima, we were met by the charismatic Roberto Plasker, C.S.C., who had served in Chile for many years before being forced to leave by the military government. He had come to Peru several years earlier. Roberto was a man of great energy and vision, whose influence was such that those who came under his care and supervision were often said to have become "Plaskerized" as a result. The programs Don McNeill developed frequently brought students into contact with the most amazing people, such as Claude-Marie Barbour in Gary and Roberto Plasker in Lima.

Lima was already a vast city overflowing with Andean migrants and a population greater than that of any of the Central American

countries we had visited. Holy Cross had just founded a parish
in a brand new squatter settlement on the northeastern edge of
Lima known as Canto Grande, where living conditions were very
harsh. The LAPEL students lived and worked in two older squatter
settlements to the south of Lima, Ciudad de Dios and Pamplona, and
traveled on Saturdays for classes with the priests in Canto Grande.
(Shortly after our time there, Henri Nouwen wrote a book about his
experiences in Ciudad de Dios and Pamplona, entitled *Gracias*.)

Roberto received us warmly, took us to the center of Lima for
a good meal and to exchange money, and then to Ciudad de Dios,
where he left us with instructions for reaching his house in Canto
Grande the following Saturday, two bus trips and two hours away
across town. He also gave us copies of Gustavo Gutiérrez's *A Theology
of Liberation* in Spanish, with the assignment to read the first chapter
before class on Saturday.

Roberto asked three things of us, each of which turned out to
be far more significant than we first realized. The first was that
we speak only Spanish. Though both Fran and I had spoken only
Spanish since leaving the United States, Spanish was still difficult.
I thought I had acquired some proficiency through language school
and three weeks of travel in Latin America, but the night we arrived
in Ciudad de Dios, we were quickly surrounded by chattering kids
who had been friends with the LAPEL students who preceded us,
and the combination of speed and slang made it impossible for me to
understand anything they were saying.

Speaking only Spanish had at least two important effects over
the months to come. The first was that we—white, college-educated,
and comparatively wealthy Americans—were much less competent
than our neighbors, who patiently helped us learn to speak Peruvian
Spanish. Our Spanish language challenges reversed, to some extent,
the social status hierarchy implied by and felt due to our origins,
education, and wealth. As a result, it was a little easier for us, from

the start, to enter into more horizontal relationships with those we encountered on a daily basis.

The second effect was that our Spanish became more fluent (though flawed), and we began to speak, work, and dream in Spanish so much that it began to feel like a more natural language for us. This allowed us to avoid two common problems experienced by those who spoke Spanish in their pastoral work and English within their own religious communities. The first of these was a linguistic bifurcation of their worlds, in which Spanish was the language of work and their language of origin was the language of friendship, relaxation, and recreation. Not bifurcating our worlds into Spanish speaking and English speaking meant one less obstacle to overcome in cross-cultural communication and in building friendships with our neighbors. The second problem it helped us avoid was speaking English in the presence of those who did not understand it, which led many to feel as if they were being intentionally or carelessly excluded, undermining trust, and creating resentment.

Roberto's second condition was that we live among the poor. He did not stipulate how we were to live, but our lodging was similar to those living around us, as was our limited access to cold water and what we had to do to feed and take care of ourselves. Unlike our neighbors, we had a safety net, and for us this manner of living was only temporary. One important result of this was that we were again—as with language—like children among adults, utterly dependent upon our neighbors to teach us the skills required for daily life: how to shop for chicken that had been squawking only minutes before, how to cook using the foods and spices available in the market, how to wash clothes by hand, how to bathe in the winter months when the water was coldest, how to get around the city by bus, and how to avoid being robbed. Once again, our neighbors were our teachers, giving us the opportunity to enter into more equal relationships with them.

Roberto's third request was that we do some useful work while we were there. He stressed that our presence for just a school year was too short to expect that we would do any great good for our neighbors. We, in turn, would be getting a great deal out of the experience—and at the very least we would become bilingual, a marketable skill—so it was only right that we try to do something useful in return. To this end, Fran and I shared two jobs, switching sites at midday. I worked at a small school for physically and mentally disabled children in the morning while Fran worked at a very large school running a library that the previous LAPEL students had gotten started. In the afternoons we switched places.

As a result of having these jobs, Fran and I gained an identity among our neighbors and an immediate connection with the families of our students. We were not just strange gringos mysteriously living in their neighborhood but teachers in the schools and—for the families of our students—the teachers of their children. They grew accustomed to seeing us walking back and forth to our two schools, while the parents of children with whom we worked began inviting us to their homes for afternoon tea and conversation.

Thus, with three simple requests Roberto created conditions favorable for our insertion into the webs of relationships with poor people in the places we lived and worked, so we could better learn from them about their own experiences, their visions of the world, and their understandings of their faith. For Roberto Plasker and the other Holy Cross priests in Canto Grande, these conditions also marked their own insertion into the communities they served and shaped their efforts to build a church in order to share the Good News with the people of Canto Grande. These priests, who would soon be joined by Holy Cross brothers and sisters, lived in very simple houses like their neighbors, without electricity, running water, sewage, paved roads, or garbage collection. Their challenge, in the words of Gustavo Gutiérrez, was how to tell these poor, marginalized, suffering women and men that God loves them.

Although the Congregation of Holy Cross had been working
in Peru since the early 1960s, they had founded Our Lord of Hope
parish in Canto Grande only two years before our arrival in 1978.
Roberto Plasker was the pastor of this parish based in a squatter
settlement of forty thousand people called Huáscar. The parish
extended to other settlements in Canto Grande and would grow
to more than two hundred thousand people in the next few years
as new settlements flooded the desert valley. These were years of
intense organizational life among the squatters in Canto Grande, as
they petitioned and pressured various government agencies to extend
necessary services to the rapidly expanding population. These were
also years of intense political life, as popular organizations brought
pressure on a weakening military regime to return to democracy and
protested against rapidly deteriorating economic conditions. Shortly
before we arrived in Peru, the military government began a transition
to democracy, holding elections for an assembly to write a new
constitution—the first elections in more than a decade. In 1980, a new
president and congress would be elected in democratic elections, and
the military would hand power back to civilian rule. The congregation
in Canto Grade was political not so much in the sense of party politics
but in that they were consistently on the side of the poor, supporting
their neighbors as they sought better living conditions and wages,
better education, and a better future for their children.

The first two months of living and working in Ciudad de Dios
were very difficult for me on many levels, and I wondered at times
whether I would have the strength to continue. I recall one day in
early October lying sick in bed, feeling miserable, and looking at
the calendar wondering how I would ever make it to May. Shortly
thereafter, however, everything began to change. Everything, from
language to work to relationships, just began to work: instead of a
fish out of water, gasping for air, I felt like a fish happily swimming
in water. Now I found myself looking at the calendar and calculating

how I might extend my stay from May to August, when I would have to return to Notre Dame for the fall semester.

One memory that stands out took place on a hot summer afternoon when I found myself alone in the priests' house in Canto Grande. I had contracted hepatitis, and, after my short hospital stay, the priests took me in so that I might recover. Some weeks passed, and they left me house-sitting during their annual community retreat. I was by myself at their house that afternoon when a woman came to the door because her baby was dying. She wanted me to baptize her little boy and pray for him. I explained that I was not a priest and I had never done anything like that before, but she insisted, and with the priests gone there was no one else to turn to. I followed the woman through a dusty maze of desert streets until we came to her shack, where family members were gathered around a bed: there, a four-month-old baby boy lay very still. Because some people confuse the sacraments with magic, I made a point of explaining that the family needed to seek medical help for her baby—knowing that there were no doctors for miles and that the family might not have enough money to pay for transportation, for the doctor, and for whatever medicines the doctor might prescribe. I then baptized Cristián in the name of the Father, the Son, and the Holy Spirit and encouraged the family to participate in the local Christian community once this crisis passed. Before I left, one of the other women present asked whether prayers could be said for her little boy, who had just died. I walked back to the priests' house, and a few minutes later a man came knocking on the door. He wanted to know whether a priest could come because they were burying his son. Death comes early to the poor, and it stays. As Gustavo used to say, the poor are on a first-name basis with death.

My spiritual life developed extraordinarily during this year as I experienced the suffering and joys of my neighbors as well as my own suffering (illness, loneliness, language and cultural frustrations, and multiple failures) and joys (discovering the Bible, language and culture acquisition, friendships, and occasional successes). In Peru that year I developed a sense of vocation, in my case not a call to ordained priesthood but a deep feeling that God was calling me to serve as a layperson among the poor. LAPEL, the space designed by Don McNeill and his gifted collaborators, had shaped my life in a powerful new direction.

My return to Notre Dame for my senior year was marked by the questions posed by this sense of vocation. Would it endure, or was it to be short-lived? If it endured, how was it to be followed? Though the priests in Canto Grande made the development of lay leadership central to their church-building efforts, there was no clear path for the participation of foreign laypersons in their ministry. How would I as a layperson find a way to serve the neighbors I had encountered in Peru?

As with any vocation, mine would require considerable discernment, testing, and deepening over the next few years. My former roommate Pepe Ahumada, who had returned to Chile where I visited him late in my LAPEL year, gave me some crucial advice: I said I wanted to dedicate myself to working with the poor in Latin America, but I had never worked with the poor in my own country. Perhaps, he suggested, I should try doing that for a time before coming back to Latin America and develop some useful skills along the way.

Fortunately for me, Don McNeill, together with others, had launched a new program that would greatly assist me in discerning my vocation to serve the poor in Peru and in developing skills that could be useful if I returned to Peru. The program they started, the Holy Cross Associates, was a postgraduate program of service, simple living, and prayer life in community that had both domestic and international sites. I applied and was accepted as a member of the first Holy Cross Associate community in Hayward, California, along with former LAPEL participants Tim Beaty, Rose Calandra, Susan Claus, and Melinda Henneberger. I worked in Parish Outreach, a parish and community organizing program sponsored by the Oakland Diocese Catholic Charities. Working in Hayward that year and in predominantly African American and Latino parishes in Oakland over the next two years, I developed many skills that served me well in later years. At home, our community life of prayer and shared meals became richer as the year went on and formed the basis for friendships that continue until this day.

Above all, this was the beginning of what would be a three-year process of discernment regarding the vocation I felt to return to Peru, during which I benefitted from retreats led by John Chaplin, C.S.C., our local director; visitors such as theologian John Dunne, C.S.C.; and John Jenkins, C.S.C., a Holy Cross seminarian studying theology in Berkeley, who served as my spiritual director. (John Jenkins would later become a professor of philosophy at Notre Dame and then Notre Dame's seventeenth president.) Through this process of discernment I discovered many things and found others beyond the reach of my understanding, but one truth became ever clearer: it was my heart's deepest desire to return to serve the poor in Peru. The question was how.

It was at this point that a providential encounter with Roberto Plasker led to an invitation from him to come to live and work with Holy Cross in Canto Grande as a layperson, and once again Don McNeill helped create a program to facilitate and support this kind of lay participation in Holy Cross's mission. The result was the Holy Cross Overseas Lay Missioner Program (the ungainly HCOLMP). At its inception, this program provided for a three-year contract with the congregation with the possibility of renewal, health insurance, and a structure of supervision and evaluation. (Years later the HCOLMP evolved into a postgraduate service program more like the Holy Cross Associates, and I was pleased to see my daughter María serve as a Holy Cross Overseas Lay Missioner for two years in Jinja, Uganda.)

It was as a Holy Cross Overseas Lay Missioner that I returned to Peru and to Canto Grande in early 1984, living in community with

Roberto Plasker, Felipe Devlin, and Arturo Colgan, who had taken over as the pastor of Our Lord of Hope parish. During my first year I worked in the school and the parish under Roberto's direction. Roberto had also formed a Holy Cross Associates program of his own, and so I was joined by three young men from Canto Grande, one of whom was married, in a special relationship with the congregation and with each other.

The following year I began working as an assistant to Arturo Colgan. The parish was growing very rapidly with new squatter settlements served by additional congregations of religious men and women from various countries. The vast parish operated in a decentralized fashion with some sixteen chapels or parish centers where the Eucharist was celebrated and teams of lay pastoral agents carried out catechesis, formed youth groups, and acted to bring the Good News to their communities. In addition to working as the pastor's assistant, I was responsible for the parish's confirmation program and I served as the advisor to a small Christian Worker's movement group in the parish.

At the same time, I began working part-time outside the parish at the Instituto Bartolomé de las Casas (IBC), founded and led by Gustavo Gutiérrez in the poor Lima district of Rímac. The IBC brought together theologians, philosophers, sociologists, economists, anthropologists, psychologists, and communications specialists to better understand the changes Peru and its people were going through, to develop better ways of serving them, and to support the theology being developed by Gustavo and his collaborators.

This marked a very rich time for me professionally, as the IBC brought me into contact with a broad network of civil society organizations and leaders, lay and religious pastoral agents, and theologians at both the national and international level. I first worked as part of a research team led by IBC director Catalina Romero, studying basic Christian communities in Peru. Later, I studied the groups leading armed insurgencies in Peru, the often bloody reaction by the state, and Christian community responses to the spiral of violence into which Peru was plunging. I taught a class at the seminary, gave talks to groups throughout Lima and in various places in Peru, and published several articles on political violence in Peru.

More importantly, in Canto Grande I met and eventually married Caridad Marchand, and over the next several years our first three children were born: Pablo, María, and Tomás. Arturo Colgan, to whom we had grown very close, presided at our wedding, joined by many other priests, including Gustavo Gutiérrez. Arturo also became the godfather of our son Pablo. (Many years later, Arturo would preside at his godson Pablo's wedding as well.) Over these years I continued to live and work in Our Lord of Hope Parish in Canto Grande, and I maintained close ties with Holy Cross. Cari and I made two visits to the United States, where we met with Don McNeill, and from time to time he visited us in Canto Grande, always taking a personal interest in our growing family.

By 1990–1991, two things had changed for us in Peru. The first was positive: my work at the IBC had led to two years of graduate study in philosophy at Peru's Catholic University, and I now felt both the need to further develop my knowledge by embarking upon studies for a doctorate and the intellectual confidence that I would be successful academically.

The second was decidedly negative. The Shining Path had been growing steadily in its capacity for violence and in instilling fear in all sectors of Peruvian society. Coupled with the violent yet apparently ineffective response by the state, Peruvians were living through an era of terror unlike any they had experienced before. Tens of thousands were already dead, and most Peruvians became dedicated to not becoming a target of the violence swirling around them. Though many doubted that the Shining Path could actually take power in Peru, it had grown without respite beyond everyone's expectations, and the question people began to ask was how many Peruvians would survive to tell the story.

The Shining Path had long been present in Canto Grande, and even during my LAPEL year they were part of the political analysis we learned from Felipe Devlin. The beginning of their armed struggle coincided with the return to democracy in 1980, and before I returned in 1984, Roberto Plasker had expelled a number of Shining Path members from one of the parish center youth groups. Shortly after I arrived, the Shining Path blew up electric transmission towers leading to Lima in a coordinated attack, plunging the entire city into darkness for many hours. When the lights went out in Canto Grande, bombs went off and a giant hammer and sickle burned in flames on the side of one of the hills. While news of massacres and mass graves in the Andes appeared in the daily newspapers, car bombs, targeted assassinations, and blackouts became everyday occurrences in Lima.

Beginning around 1990, the Shining Path became much more aggressive with respect to the church. They began a campaign of assassinations and intimidation of church personnel, martyring two women religious and three priests in the space of a year. In Canto Grande there were both diffuse and specific threats to church personnel, accompanied by the killing of a police officer in front of the main parish office and the bombing of two bank offices just around the corner, as well as the bombing of a police cruiser. Infiltration, takeovers, and attempted takeovers of popular organizations and unions, flash mobs of a hundred or so Shining Path militants marching through markets and main thoroughfares, and reports of nighttime training for the takeover of Lima taking place in some of the secondary schools were all common. At home in bed we heard the sounds of gunfire many nights as the Peruvian military enforced a curfew and set up roadblocks into Canto Grande, firing their weapons as a means of intimidation of their own. We lived in fear, a fear accentuated in my case as I had become the IBC's principal analyst of the Shining Path and I was acutely aware of what they were doing throughout the country.

This powerful negative push factor and the positive pull factor of doctoral studies both pointed in the same direction: a temporary move to the United States for doctoral studies. Once again, Don McNeill played a central role in shaping my life, interceding with authorities at Notre Dame to facilitate my admission to the doctoral program in political science.

As if to mark the gravity of the situation, in the weeks leading up to our departure, the Shining Path shot one priest, who luckily survived, but a few days later killed two other priests. The most bizarre incident took place the morning we were to fly to the United States. We hired a van and driver to take us, our luggage, and various family members to the airport to see us off. Very early that morning the van stopped first to pick up family members who lived a little farther up the valley than we did. When the van reached the intersection of the main road that led to our house and to the airport, they found the intersection blocked by flames lighting the predawn darkness. A group of young people surrounded the van, and a somewhat older man stepped forward to interrogate the van driver. After a brief exchange of words, the driver decided to make a run for it and stepped on the gas, escaping—but not before the young people had punctured two of the tires and smashed several of the van's windows. This seems to have been a training exercise for the Shining Path takeover of Lima and had nothing to do with us personally, but the van had barely escaped being burned, and our family members were badly shaken. There was a twenty-four-hour tire repair shop near our house, so with only some delay we were able to make it to the airport on time for our flight, broken windows and all. We felt at that moment like Jews fleeing Germany just before the Holocaust, our relief tempered by our concern for the safety of the family, friends, and colleagues we were leaving behind.

Doctoral studies at Notre Dame marked a new phase in our relationship with Don McNeill, as I was no longer part of a program he had designed or mentored, and he quickly became our family's best friend. Our children grew up with the familiar presence of Padre Donaldo, or "Don Alto" as he sometimes said, and he often treated us to a trip to Subway and a visit to his dorm room. Don was especially attentive to Caridad, for whom the move to Notre Dame—away from her family, her career, and the only language she knew—was the most difficult. Don would often take Cari out for a beer, just to talk, and just as he had helped me many times, he helped her attend an intensive English language program in Chicago our first summer at Notre Dame. Don was with us in good times and in bad, and when Andrés, our fourth child, was born while we lived in University Village at Notre Dame, it was only natural that Don would become his godfather—a role he had long before assumed. (It might please Don to know that his godchild is serving in the Jesuit Volunteer Corp in San Antonio after graduating from college.)

Although we moved away from Notre Dame in 1997 so that I could take an academic position at the University of Oklahoma, we have remained in close contact with Don at Notre Dame, in Chicago, and back again at Notre Dame. And Don McNeill was not done shaping our lives. For a number of years we drove from Oklahoma to Deer Park, Maryland, every summer where Don organized a retreat for his confreres and for those like our family who had been involved in some kind of service opportunity with Holy Cross. We met many wonderful families and reconnected with old friends such as Jim and Maryanne Roemer and John Dunne, C.S.C., praying and reflecting together while also enjoying recreating with our families.

My children are grateful for Don's loving presence in their lives and for teaching them to play pool at Deer Park and to quack like ducks in his dorm. Caridad is deeply appreciative of his constant friendship and attentive kindness over the past thirty years. I simply cannot conceive

of what my life would have been without Don McNeill, and I give
thanks for him in the way I give thanks for my parents, without whom
I would not be. Grateful for Don's friendship, inspired by his vision,
and a witness to how he changed my life as well as the lives of so many
others, I try in small ways to follow his example. I write these words
today in Lima, Peru, just having said good-bye to nineteen University
of Oklahoma students who participated in the Journey to Latin
America–Peru, an experiential learning study-abroad program I led.
After several weeks of preparation in the United States, students come
to Peru to encounter its people in all their diversity. After spending time
in Lima on Peru's Pacific Coast, visiting Machu Picchu and peasant
communities high in the Andes, and taking boats upriver deep into the
Amazonian rain forest with local indigenous guides, I asked this year's
students to name the most important memory they would take away
from their month in Peru. More than any other experience, they chose
their encounters with the people of Canto Grande. *Gracias, Donaldo.*

CHAPTER 11

Holy Cross in Uganda:
Living the Lay Vocation Theologically

Paul Mitchell

*A*s an undergraduate, I could have been fairly characterized as a sucker for experiential learning. I loved traveling to new places and learning at every moment from people committed to meaningful work. I spent my college summers at a national park in Costa Rica, a summer camp in Utah, and schools of popular education in rural El Salvador. I studied abroad in Mexico; spent three spring breaks on justice seminars in Washington, DC, and Chicago; and spent many nights at the Catholic Worker House. I listened to many stories.

Not surprisingly, as a second-semester senior, I found myself awash in other people's life paths and passions. I felt skilled at listening and learning, not narrowing on one life path and committing to it. As a result, a feeling of dull panic marked my final months of college. I felt as though I lacked the ability to make a prudent decision about where to commit the first full-time steps of my vocation.

During this time, one of my roommates, Michael, was entering formation to become a Jesuit priest. He was to enter the "novitiate," a school of the heart that would allow him to enter more deeply into his interior life in order to listen for and live his vocation. The novitiate represented two years of prayerful solitude and work "experiments" while living in a community of peers and wise interlocutors.

Honestly, I was jealous of Michael. While I did not feel drawn to enter priestly formation, I did yearn for a similar growth toward depth in prayer and vocation. I wanted to know which path fit the contours of my passion and ability. I wanted a novitiate for laypeople.

Since such a thing did not exist, I searched for a postgraduate service program that seemed to approximate the experience. This is when I talked to Tom Smith, C.S.C., then the head of the Holy Cross Mission Center, about living with the Holy Cross in East Africa. He told me about the OLM (Overseas Lay Missioner) program, where a group of volunteers would live proximate to a parish community and a formation house in eastern Uganda. While the volunteers would begin work at a secondary school, Tom assured me that there would be flexibility to search for a work placement that one was drawn to. If the C.S.C. in Uganda were anything like Tom, there would be good company on this journey. Solitude. Experiments in vocation. Good company. All of this sounded like a solid lay novitiate experience to me.

So I signed the contract, and in the fall of 2007, I was sent by the Congregation of Holy Cross to eastern Uganda. I found myself living in Bugembe, a semirural truck stop town on the road that stretched from Kampala east toward Kenya, in a little orange house with six other recent Notre Dame graduates. While my decision seemed a sound one, the reality of my two years in Uganda was notably messy. It was precisely this messiness that marked my lay novitiate and made it proper lay formation.

One evening, as we approached graduation, a group of friends and I asked Fr. Paul Kollman, C.S.C., what he considered the "greatest challenge of our generation." His answer was the "cultivation of solitude." Largely an overzealous bunch formed at the Center for

Social Concerns, our reactions ranged from skeptical acceptance to muffled horror. Didn't this guy know about the urgency of the struggle for justice?

Of course Paul knew. But he also knew that without solitude we could not become centered within ourselves, access the grace of our lives, share this graced life with another person, and authentically build a community worthy of the trust needed to withstand the significant challenges of our age.

He offered the image of an empty glass. The empty glass represented the time and interior bandwidth available in one day. One can fill up the glass with only a finite number of marbles. The big marbles, priorities, go in first, and the little marbles fill in the space left around the sides. "I've made the decision," Paul explained, "that solitude and prayer simply must go into the glass first."

With all the distractions that university life offered, I found it difficult to prioritize solitude. But that fall, my life in Uganda offered significantly fewer choices to fill my days. It was as though the big "solitude" marble had been chosen for me. Access to the Internet was scarce, hand-washing laundry was meditative, and a thirty-minute walk through a beautiful countryside with a view of Lake Victoria was the daily commute.

Easy, right? Did I gain that interior wisdom that I so longed for? Hardly. As a twenty-three-year-old formed to think of myself as someone who must change the world, rural Uganda is a difficult place to land. There is just not that much to "do." My journal entries from our first days in Uganda pulsate with a visceral craving to feel like I am doing, achieving, learning. Our arrival was not anticipated at the schools we were told that we would work at, and without command of the local language, for us meaningful work was hard to come by.

In the spiritual classic *Addiction and Grace*, Gerald May argues that we are in need of grace, but, impatient, we try to substitute this unearned love with something that we can control. Soon, we develop a compulsive attachment to this substitution. This addicted behavior fills our hands such that it is difficult to receive the infinite grace woven into our lives.

Solitude, in my experience, quickly lays bare this compulsive behavior. Thomas Merton names my particular compulsion with devastating accuracy.

> There is a pervasive form of contemporary violence to which the idealist most easily succumbs: activism and overwork. The rush and pressure of modern life are a form, perhaps the most common form, of its innate violence. To allow oneself to be carried away by a multitude of conflicting concerns, to surrender to too many demands, to commit oneself to too many projects, to want to help everyone in everything, is to succumb to violence. The frenzy of our activism neutralizes our work for peace. It destroys our own inner capacity for peace. It destroys the fruitfulness of our own work, because it kills the root of inner wisdom which makes work fruitful.[139]

Solitude, then, affords the clarity to look at the compulsive behavior that we substitute for the grace of our lives. I sensed the hollowness of my compulsion and began to search within myself. It is an odd feeling to travel to the other side of the world only to feel the gravitational pull of books on how to access and integrate my interior life. But pull they did, and I began to search. As I learned the contours of my interior life, I returned often to a quote that a friend wrote inside a journal that she gifted me as I left for Uganda. It is the following from Etty Hillesum:

139 Merton, *Conjectures of a Guilty Bystander*, 73.

With all the suffering there is, you begin to feel
ashamed of taking yourself and your moods so seriously.
But you must continue to take yourself seriously.
You must remain your own witness, marking well
everything that happens in this world, never shutting
your eyes to reality. You must come to grips with these
terrible times and try to find answers to the many
questions these pose. And perhaps the answers will help
not only yourself but also others.[140]

This quote helped me contextualize my inner search within my
development as someone who desired to do meaningful justice work.
Learning the contours of my inner life is an indispensible part of the
formation of enduring discipleship.

So, what did I learn? Once I was able to settle down, I was able
to receive the love that my neighbors were offering. The best way
that I can think to describe this love is that of the "abiding" love that
Jesus evokes in the Gospel of John. This Greek verb (*menó*) denotes a
continuity of presence and an endurance of condition. This is the love
that I encountered in Uganda.

To be clear, this is *not* the love I thought that I was signing
up for. I had just spent three consecutive summers in El Salvador.
There, I found a muscular, revolutionary love. I learned community
organizing and popular education from ex-guerillas. I learned about
a prophetic church from a generation formed by Oscar Romero. The
people shared their stories openly, and, since I spoke the language
fluently, I was able to learn at every moment.

The world I encountered in eastern Uganda felt like an entire
planet away from Central America. I had traded the revolutionary
fervor of *la lucha* (struggle) for a life marked by the mantra of

---

140 Hillesum, *An Interrupted Life: The Diaries, 1941–1943; and Letters from Westerbork*, 41.

mpola, mpola (slowly, slowly). At first, I resented that there was not much to do other than abide in this love. I adjusted but with considerable difficulty. When I had tuned to the place, I found deep presence in the personalities around me.

One unforgettable personality was that of Agapetus, a seminarian in the Congregation of Holy Cross. An unlikely alpha male of the formation house, Aga boasted the self-proclaimed nickname of "the Bouncer" while weighing just shy of one hundred pounds. I first met him as he stormed up and down the sidelines coaching his peers on the seminary soccer team. This is where he showed his love and also cloaked his total inability to play sports. Later that day, he bestowed us all with nicknames (I was "Letters"—as in "The Letters of St. Paul"), and he made us feel welcome immediately.

One day, as I was walking home from town, I was overtaken by a group of the Holy Cross seminarians riding their bikes. Aga was among them and refused to let me walk, beckoning me to ride on the rack over the back tire of his bike. This rack, made of thin metal, did not inspire confidence. Sensing my worry, he assured me that he was able to transport the "fattest people in my village" on that same bike rack. With that endorsement, I reluctantly hopped on, and we took off down the hill toward home. This is a curious story of companionship, with my white knuckles digging into Agapetus Mukabane's cheap bike rack, but it is an illustrative example of the type of love that I encountered. Agapetus did not want my revolution. He wanted to know whether I trusted him enough to be along for the ride. Once I earned this trust, then the building might follow, but the trust born of "abiding" was primary.

When I had been studying at Notre Dame, my course readings often invoked references to the "baptismal call to discipleship," the "priesthood of all believers," and the "universal call to holiness." While it would take me a few Google searches to locate these quotes within the documents of Vatican II, the meaning I drew was the following: even though I did not feel drawn to "religious life," I could still live an authentically *religious life*, listening for the evolving desire that God weaves into my heart and taking the risk to live and to build out of that desire.

I found myself awash in others' stories of passionate service. I just had no focused idea of which mode of life or heart's passion the mystery of God wished to speak through me. And I also sensed that desire does not exist in a vacuum. It must be incarnated in the context of some need and calibrated with my ability. I knew that I needed an "experimental" approach to work. I needed to test out a mode of life, test the fit, recalibrate, and repeat.

Thankfully, I was put in an unfamiliar place where it was possible to seek these experiments. Tom Smith made it clear that I would begin teaching at the Holy Cross secondary school and, from there, discern a best-fit work placement.

When we landed, we were met warmly by the Holy Cross but with awkward neglect. The secondary school did not have classes scheduled for us for the upcoming semester. (If a current volunteer had not given up his eighth-grade-equivalent "computer theory" class to me, I would have been out of work entirely.) It quickly became clear that there was no one in the congregation who was going to curate our work. If we were going to find meaningful work, we had to ask for what we wanted.

To be clear, I do not understand this neglect from the congregation to be malicious. There was simply no one with the time and ability to translate the unique exuberance of a twenty-three-year-old who has been told repeatedly to be the change he wants to see in the world. There were days when I resented this lack of guidance, but in retrospect, I judge that it was almost imprudent for me to expect this. The situation also introduced me to a generative question for the reality of the lay church. Why was I waiting on priests to tell me how to live out of my baptism? Was I not capable of listening to my passion and ability and carve out meaningful work?

I arrived in Uganda with a passion for formative education. I had studied in schools of popular education and political formation in El Salvador. I read all the Paulo Freire that I could get my hands on. It was a rude awakening, then, when I found myself being asked to teach a computer theory class where sixty students mechanically took notes while I parroted an outdated history of the computer. It turned out to be a comically poor fit.

After about a month, I begged into a meeting with the rector of the "Philosophy Centre–Jinja" (PCJ), the little junior college/seminary hybrid where the seminarians from the Holy Cross and other missionary orders study English, philosophy, and social science in an undergraduate-like maturation phase. I loved the school, and I asked whether I could be a teaching assistant.

In a gesture of extraordinary trust, the rector offered me the chance to teach one social science elective per semester. After I shook the rector's arm out of his socket in thanks for the offer, I spent hours over the next month cobbling together the syllabi for my courses out of my undergraduate studies of "the great books" and peace studies. My favorite course that I taught was on "understanding power." We read theories of political and economic power, discussed readings on power, race, gender, and why this language matters for people of faith.

I aimed to make the class a "seminar" style, where the students took over the discussion and felt free to challenge a reading that I assigned or a point that I made. However, this style was quite foreign to public secondary education in East Africa. The deference to perceived authority in East Africa is nearly total, and authority is conferred by, among other things, the position of "teacher" and of advanced age.

This allowed my class to be in the rare position of the disruption of assumed authority. Yes, I was their teacher, but they were also my same age, plus or minus three years. They took me seriously as an instructor but felt free, given our proximity in age, to think freely and to challenge. I had walked into a disruptive authority sweet spot.

I loved teaching at the PCJ, and this would never have happened if I had not asked. This experience, for me, highlighted the significant freedom we have as lay disciples. There is no vow of obedience and no "role" bound by another people's view of clericalism. I have the ability to perceive the passion blooming in my interior life and my ability to cocreate with God. This takes imagination and initiative, but the creative space is ours for the taking.

This freedom, however, must be taught and tempered by perception of expectations and social intelligence. Just because I do not have the expectations put on me that priests do does not mean I can forget these expectations altogether. I learned this lesson rather decisively in the following conflict at the parish.

When the PCJ was not in session, I again began feeling the compulsion to *do* and began working at the HIV/AIDS outreach at the parish. The bulk of the work was to organize voluntary counseling and testing outreach. We were assigned to offer people the opportunity to know their HIV status and to refer the infected to treatment centers. Entering this work, I thought of myself as possessing above-average listening skills and social intelligence. Still, I was gripped by this desire to *do*, and this limited my vision of a tangle of unspoken assumptions and historical fault lines within the parish and the congregation. Overzealous, I waded right into a conflict that I did not fully perceive regarding authority, power, and money.

These conflicts culminated in my invitation to a parish leadership meeting and being loudly and unceremoniously fired. To be clear, my dismissal was definitely the best thing given my misperception of the situation. Just because I eagerly wished well did not mean that I was effectively serving.

My compulsion to *do* actually impaired my ability to do so. The experience of failure at work caused me significant pain. As a human being, I am a compulsive banisher of pain. When confronted with a painful situation, my reaction is "This hurts! It must be bad!

Get it away from me!" I will then try to run or rationalize it away. The prayerful solitude, though, gave me the courage to stay with the struggle and pain, attend to it, and cultivate the trust and hope in life on the other side of the pain.

For me, the message on the other side of the pain was one of patience and prudence. In the parish, who were the rightful protagonists, the leaders who could actually undermine the injustice that we saw? Was I really the rightful protagonist? Just because I could claim the authority in the situation, should I have? I think this is a generative theme for exuberant "world changers." When are you the protagonist, and when do you need to get out of the way?

My work "experiments" introduced me to the ambivalence of authority that confronts a layperson who wants to live deeply into his or her baptism. I am not a priest, and so I am not beholden to the "role" and expectations that people place on clergy. I am also not held accountable by a superior to remain attentive to my heart's desire and remain true to it. Also, since I am not a priest, I do not come with the built-in credibility/audience. Additionally, I still must remain attentive to the reality that priests find themselves in and work within this reality. These contours have to be acknowledged since their negotiation shapes this free space of lay creation.

I have found that negotiating this ambivalence demands good company. While my relationship with the Holy Cross in Uganda was primarily one of neglect during my time in Uganda, men and women of the Congregation of the Holy Cross have walked with me since that experience to help me live into my vocation.

Leaving Uganda, I spent two months in Bangladesh. (The woman whom I was in love with and am now married to was working in and around Dhaka.) In Bangladesh, I found Tom McDermott, C.S.C., who had spent most of his life as a priest in East Africa. He was thus able to offer context on the struggles and politics that existed within the church there. Decisively extroverted,

Tom repeatedly interrupted my silent retreat that year with tours of the city and a talk to the summer volunteers on the topic "the Truth will make you strange." Tom's ability to imagine and build out of that imagination with enviable exuberance is still a reminder to me to get outside of myself.

After Bangladesh, I settled in Chicago and began the process of integrating my experience while beginning to build a career in the United States. Under the pressure of this challenge, I often lost focus on the lessons of "abiding" and prayerful solitude that I learned in Uganda, and I rather flailed through my midtwenties. From that time until the present, Judith Anne Beattie, C.S.C., has been a remarkably attentive spiritual director, helping me to return continually to the truth of my life and the love of a merciful God. I know that I need good company to maintain endurance in prayerful solitude and cultivating an experimental attitude toward work.

I am convinced that laypeople in the church need to cultivate prayerful solitude and an experimental attitude toward work in order to live out of a cultivated inner authority into a faithful vocation. But what is the terrain like that we must accomplish this in? Is it more like a garden or a forest? Gardens are tended, cropped, and domesticated. Forests are undomesticated, teeming with life, and disorientingly immense.

My time in Uganda was unequivocally a forest. The uncertainty and complexity were significant, but this is precisely the terrain that a faithful layperson must inhabit. I often wonder whether, in my search for a lay novitiate, I was seeking the safety of a garden. In the anxiety of leaving college, I felt tempted by the sneaky compulsion to conform to a known story, to someone else's path. (Frankly, I still feel the tug of this compulsion.) More and more, I believe that gardens, these domesticated spaces of formation, are, in themselves, domesticating. Yes, gardens of formation are right for a certain stage, but the lay vocation is lived in the forest, so we must build formation opportunities that deal with modern disorientation and fragmentation.

As a baptized person, I am coming to see the disorienting immensity and complexity of the forest of the world. This is the place where we must live life, and to leave this forest is to shirk the cross of the lay vocation. With prayerful solitude, experiments in vocation, and good company we can (and must) build the structures that support enduring lay vocation in the church.

Afterword

Fr. Paul Kollman, C.S.C.

The Constitutions of the Congregation of Holy Cross urge members of the male part of the Holy Cross family—priests, brothers, and those in formation—to be "men with hope to bring" (Constitution 8, para. 118). This collection of essays honoring Fr. Don McNeill, C.S.C., and celebrating his generative ministry proclaims vividly Don's capacity to be such a hope bringer—both by his personal accompaniment and through the fruitfulness of his role as a builder of institutions such as the Center for Social Concerns. Each of the contributors describes walking the path of discipleship with Don (or with those inspired by him) in ways that have been formative and transformative. Each has found in Don someone who catalyzed a discovery of new horizons of possibility in a challenged and ultimately deepened faith, often through intimate encounters with human suffering. The essays themselves thus represent, I believe, another source of hope—a written one—since they testify to not only Don's capacity but also that of the other contributors, as women and men with hope to bring.

It is my earnest prayer that those who read these essays will have found new wellsprings of hope with which to guide their lives. Thus, Don's spirit present in this these essays from among his many friends will continue to open new horizons.

Reading these essays has prompted in me, first, a profound feeling of gratitude; second, a heightened sense of responsibility; and, third, a renewed commitment to the spirit of accompaniment and collaboration that has marked Don's ministry.

I am grateful to my friends Margie Pfeil and Don McNeill for their work in organizing this collection. I thank, too, all of the contributors for the loving work of remembering, analyzing, writing—and no doubt laughing and sometimes crying—as these essays took their shape. Many of the essays evoke very personal experiences, some of them embarrassing to recall, and place those experiences within both a precious individual life and a larger programmatic vision about how education of mind and heart can occur.

The moving personal self-revelations that mark these essays powerfully enact the pastoral-theological instincts of Don McNeill himself. Early on, Don learned to trust what the Nobel Prize–winning poet Czesław Miłosz once called "the immense call of the Particular,"[141] a trust and invitation echoed in the works of Henri Nouwen and our late Holy Cross brother John Dunne. Don believes a crucial theological task is to take personal experience seriously. And thus he has long invited students and colleagues—perhaps most importantly at the Center for Social Concerns—to do the hard work of paying attention: letting experiences speak, plumbing the depths of memory, and engagement with suffering for images and

---

141 The poem is called "Capri" (Czesław Miłosz, *Facing the River*, trans. Robert Haas and author: 1995, 9ff).

insights speaking of sin and grace as well as the human and Christian mysteries of creation, incarnation, passion, death, and resurrection. Each essay breathes a deep respect for Providence guiding such reflective theological work, so that, again recalling Miłosz, we learn this painful yet redemptive truth:

> Now I know foolishness is necessary in all our designs,
> so that they are realized, awkwardly and incompletely.[142]

Thank you, Margie, Don, and all contributors, for sharing your journeys so honestly.

Along with gratitude, I feel a deep sense of responsibility. First, I feel this as a Holy Cross priest seeing what one of us has accomplished in his rich life. Second, and more personally, I feel particularly responsible to continue Don's work and the spirit in which he did it as the third director of the Center for Social Concerns—a Notre Dame treasure that Don nurtured and guided, a place and community that proudly seeks to embody Don's vision for the rich possibilities of a Notre Dame education. Several contributors are valued colleagues at the CSC itself or elsewhere at Notre Dame, while others carry the CSC's vision in practices of education and justice seeking they pursue elsewhere.

I knew little of the CSC or its precursors when I was a Notre Dame undergraduate in the early 1980s. Later as a seminarian, however, I came to deeply admire what I learned about the CSC, and my first teaching role came as a coinstructor in the class Don helped develop, Theology and Community Service. With guides such as Don, Andrea Smith Shappell, and Ann Seckinger, I learned

---

142 Ibid.

the value of education combining intimate encounters with human suffering, close attention to personal responses to it, investigation of social causes for marginalization, and critical theological reflection guided by the Catholic social tradition. This is a pedagogy we value at the Center for Social Concerns to this day, and I embrace the responsibility of maintaining and, where possible, improving it as we learn more about its promises for transformative education more than three decades after the CSC's founding.

Finally, reading these essays reaffirmed my commitment to the collaborative spirit that has always embodied Don McNeill's ministry. The essayists, along with others whom they mention, represent some of Don's closest companions in his ministerial life, yet there are many others unnamed with whom he has walked the path of discipleship, learned the ways of compassion, embraced the cross of Christ, and known the power of the resurrection. Such zeal for collaboration—including a remarkable capacity to welcome those who disagreed with him—was a hallmark of Don's leadership at the Center for Social Concerns.

I draw strength from Don's example as I seek to welcome the same spirit, struggling always for the patience that marks his life and ministry.

A poem by Derek Walcott, another Nobel Prize–winning poet, entitled "Love after Love,"[143] has inspired me and speaks to me of the gratitude, responsibility, and renewed commitment I feel in light of Don McNeill's ministry as captured in these essays:

---

143 http://www.poemhunter.com/poem/love-after-love/. Accessed August 19, 2016.

The time will come
when, with elation,
you will greet yourself arriving
at your own door, in your own mirror,
and each will smile at the other's welcome,

and say, sit here. Eat.
You will love again the stranger who was your self.
Give wine. Give bread. Give back your heart
to itself, to the stranger who has loved you

all your life, whom you ignored
for another, who knows you by heart.
Take down the love letters from the bookshelf,

the photographs, the desperate notes,
peel your own image from the mirror.
Sit. Feast on your life.

Don McNeill has welcomed so many into the process of self-discovery Walcott describes. In this process, the inevitable alienation from ourselves is overcome—always partially, as in a mirror, but nonetheless really—by grace-inspired encounters with others. These are, in a Christian idiom, Eucharistic encounters in which we are broken and shared, able better to feast on all that divine love pours into our lives as we delve into the "love letters from the bookshelf, the photographs, the desperate notes."

Thank you, Don, for the feasts to which you have welcomed so many, and to the contributors to this volume, who open up more seats at the ever-abundant table of life, ours and others'.

Biographies of Contributors

SR. JUDITH ANNE BEATTIE, C.S.C., was one of the founding members of the Center for Social Concerns. Serving as assistant director of the center, Judith Anne supervised the service learning component of the center. For this work, she received the Grenville Clark award in 1981, and, together with Don McNeill, she received a Special Presidential Award from Fr. Hesburgh in 1983. Her past ministries in Holy Cross have been in health care, formation ministry, and leadership in the area of North America. Currently, Judith Anne is involved in spiritual direction and retreat ministry along with directing the program that prepares young women in Holy Cross for final commitment.

WILLIAM T. CAVANAUGH, PHD, is professor of Catholic studies and director of the Center for World Catholicism and Intercultural Theology at DePaul University. He was a Holy Cross associate in Colorado Springs in 1984–1985 and in Chile in 1987–1989. His degrees are from the universities of Notre Dame, Cambridge, and Duke. He is the author of seven books and editor of three more. His books and articles have been published in eleven languages. He is married and has three sons.

MATT FEENEY is the chairman of Snell & Wilmer, a law firm based in the western United States, with offices in Arizona, California, Nevada, Utah, Colorado, and Los Cabos, Mexico. Matt graduated from the University of Notre Dame in 1979 and from Notre Dame Law School in 1983. He served in Phoenix as a Holy Cross Associate in 1979–1980, teaching at St. Matthew Catholic School. He and his wife, Michele, have five children and have lived in Phoenix since they graduated from Notre Dame Law School.

BARBARA FREY is director of the Human Rights Program in the College of Liberal Arts at the University of Minnesota. The program, established in 2001, provides academic, research, and internship opportunities for students in the field of international human rights. She attended the University of Notre Dame (BA, 1978) and the University of Wisconsin Law School (JD, 1982).

STACY HENNESSY is a native of Louisville, Kentucky. After graduating from the University of Notre Dame in 1981, she went to Chile with the Holy Cross Associates. Upon her return she spent time working with the developmentally disabled. Later she moved to Boston, where she lived at the Catholic Worker House while completing a master's degree in theology at Weston School of Theology. She has since worked in campus ministry at Iona College and in several high schools. She is married, has two children, and is currently teaching at Brebeuf Jesuit in Indianapolis. Prior to this book, she collaborated with Fr. Don McNeill, C.S.C., on the books *Compassion* and *Doing the Truth in Love*.

CHARLES D. KENNEY, PHD, is the husband of Caridad Marchand and the father of Pablo, María, Tomás, and Andrés. He received a BA in philosophy and an MA and PhD in political science from the University of Notre Dame. He has taught democratization and Latin American politics at the University of Oklahoma and been an active member of St. Thomas More University Parish since 1997. His academic publications focus on politics in Peru and Latin America; he was a Fulbright Fellow in Peru, served as an international elections observer, and chaired the Peru Section of the Latin American Studies Association.

FR. PAUL KOLLMAN, C.S.C., became the third executive director of the Center for Social Concerns in July 2012. He is an associate professor in the Department of Theology and is a fellow of the Helen Kellogg Institute for International Studies, the Joan B. Kroc Institute for International Peace Studies, and the Nanovic Institute for European Studies at the University of Notre Dame. His research focuses on African Christianity, mission history, and world Christianity. Father Kollman received his BA and MDiv degrees from the University of Notre Dame and his doctorate from the University of Chicago Divinity School.

MARY ELLEN KONIECZNY, PHD, is associate professor of sociology and Henkels Family Collegiate Chair at the University of Notre Dame. After her HCA year, she earned an MDiv from Weston Jesuit School of Theology (1985) and worked in ministry and administration for the Archdiocese of Chicago. She received her PhD in sociology from the University of Chicago in 2005. She is interested in the complex relationship between religion and conflict, and her book *The Spirit's Tether: Family, Work, and Religion among American Catholics* (OUP 2013) examines how religion and family life support and shape Catholic Americans' moral and political polarization. She is presently working on a book on religious conflicts in the US military.

FR. DON MCNEILL, C.S.C., ND '58, entered the Congregation of Holy Cross in 1959 and was ordained a priest in 1966. After earning a doctorate in pastoral theology at Princeton University, he returned to Notre Dame, where he founded the Center for Experiential Learning and later the Center for Social Concerns in 1983, serving as executive director until 2002. Thereafter, he was a senior fellow at Notre Dame's Institute for Latino Studies in its Metropolitan Chicago Initiative, assisting in pastoral work at St. Ann's parish in the Pilsen neighborhood. He recently celebrated his eightieth birthday and his fiftieth anniversary of ordination.

PAUL MITCHELL graduated from Notre Dame in 2007 from the Program of Liberal Studies. Since then, he has worked as a teacher and teacher coach in Jinja, Uganda; Cairo, Egypt; Chicago; and Boston. He studied theology and education at the School of Theology and Ministry at Boston College. At the moment, Paul is stepping back from full-time classroom teaching as he anticipates becoming the primary caregiver to his and his wife's first child. He is learning Web development and is exploring the intersection of online communities, remote education, and lay formation.

LOUIS M. NANNI is serving in his fifteenth year as vice president for University Relations at the University of Notre Dame. Lou previously served for eight years as executive director of the Center for the Homeless in South Bend, Indiana. He received a bachelor's degree from Notre Dame in 1984 and for two years following graduation served as a lay missioner in a Santiago, Chile, shantytown. He then entered Notre Dame's international peace studies program, earning a master's degree in 1988. He and his wife, Carmen, a 1993 Notre Dame graduate, have five children.

FELICIA JOHNSON O'BRIEN, ND '95, helped start the Farm of the Child in Honduras, an orphanage she continues to support as a board member. For four years, she oversaw international recruitment efforts at Notre Dame. She then pursued her master's in social work at the Catholic University of America, where she focused on working with immigrants and refugees. Johnson O'Brien joined the staff at the Center for Social Concerns in 2008 to help coordinate the Summer Service Learning Program (SSLP).

MAUREEN R. O'BRIEN, PHD, is associate professor of theology at Duquesne University in Pittsburgh, Pennsylvania. She researches and writes on topics including practical theology and the identity and reflective practices of Catholic lay ministers. She edited (with Susan Yanos) *Emerging from the Vineyard: Essays by Lay Ecclesial Ministers* (Fortuity, 2014). Prior to working in parish ministry and completing graduate studies at Boston College, she earned her bachelor's degree at the University of Notre Dame in theology. There she was active in the Community for the International Lay Apostolate (CILA) and worked at the Center for Experiential Learning.

MARGARET R. PFEIL, PHD, ND '87, '97, '00, was a Holy Cross associate in Chile, 1987–1989, and now holds a joint appointment in the Department of Theology and in the Center for Social Concerns at the University of Notre Dame, where she is also a faculty fellow of the Kroc Institute for International Peace Studies. She is a cofounder and resident of the St. Peter Claver Catholic Worker Community in South Bend, Indiana.

MARY ANN ROEMER worked with Fr. Don McNeill and Sr. Judith Anne Beattie, C.S.C., to establish the Office of Volunteer Services at the University of Notre Dame in 1976 and was part of the founding staff of the Center for Social Concerns, where she continued to accompany students for twenty years. She focused in particular on cultivating the hospitality dimension of the CSC, and in this work, she often collaborated with her husband, Jim, who served as Notre Dame's dean of student affairs for ten years.

ANDREA SMITH SHAPPELL, ND, '79, '81 MA, has worked at the Center for Social Concerns for thirty-five years in a variety of positions such as teaching with Don McNeill, C.S.C.; advising students about postgraduate service; and directing the Summer Service Learning Program. Andrea and her husband, Brian, continued the formation started in CILA by serving with the Social Apostolate of the Archdiocese of New Orleans in 1980–1981. They are grateful that their children, Elizabeth, Eric, and Nicholas, engaged in the courses and programs of the Center for Social Concerns while students at Notre Dame.

Acknowledgments

This book is the fruit of many generous hearts and spirits. In particular, we would like to thank Kathy and Hugh Andrews as well as Kirsty Melville of Andrews McMeel Universal in facilitating the publishing process. To the McNeill and Heck families, we extend our deep gratitude for their steady support and generosity. We are so grateful to our colleagues and friends at the Center for Social Concerns for their encouragement along the way. Finally, we offer a special thanks to our editor, Jean Lucas, for her gentle patience in guiding this project to completion.

Andrews McMeel Publishing
a division of Andrews McMeel Universal
1130 Walnut Street, Kansas City, Missouri 64106

www.andrewsmcmeel.com

16 17 18 19 20 RR2 10 9 8 7 6 5 4 3 2 1

ISBN: 978-1-4494-8203-9

Library of Congress Control Number: 2016951820

Editor: Jean Z. Lucas
Designer: Holly Swayne
Art Director: Tim Lynch
Production Manager: Cliff Koehler
Production Editor: Maureen Sullivan

Cover art: Adapted from a scarf created by Debra Boyette in the
Silk Creations Program at St. Margaret's House, South Bend, Indiana

ATTENTION: SCHOOLS AND BUSINESSES
Andrews McMeel books are available at quantity
discounts with bulk purchase for educational, business, or
sales promotional use. For information, please e-mail the
Andrews McMeel Publishing Special Sales Department:
specialsales@amuniversal.com.